The America I Once Knew—
Vanishing But Not
Forgotten

The America I Once Knew— Vanishing But Not Forgotten

A World War II Veteran Takes a Critical View of the Foibles of American Society

Chuck Salm

Writers Club Press

New York Lincoln Shanghai

The America I Once Knew—Vanishing But Not Forgotten
A World War II Veteran Takes a Critical View of the Foibles of American Society

Writers Club Press
an imprint of iUniverse, Inc.

For information address:
iUniverse, Inc.
2021 Pine Lake Road, Suite 100
Lincoln, NE 68512
www.iuniverse.com

ISBN: 0-595-25670-8 (pbk)
ISBN: 0-595-65247-6 (cloth)

Printed in the United States of America

Man must be arched and buttressed from within; else the temple wavers to the dust.

—Marcus Aurelius

Contents

Acknowledgments xi

Prologue xiii

To the Reader xvii

Terrorism and the Challenge We Face xxi

CHAPTER 1   Doctrine of Confusion 1

* *Senior Citizens, How Sweet It Is* *1*
* *The Case for Cynicism.* *2*
* *When We Go to the Polls, Consider How We Look to the Outside World* *6*
* *An Affront To Decency* *7*
* *This is Your FBI* *8*
* *Immigration and the Impact on our Environment.* *9*
* *Joe College!—And Betty Co-ed, Too!* *10*
* *Gun Nuts, The NRA & Politicians* *11*
* *The Demise of Reason* *12*
* *The Calamity of Negligence* *14*

CHAPTER 2   To Have or Have Not 19

* *The Rich, The Ultra-Rich, The Hungry and the Hurting* *19*
* *It's Great to Have Charisma* *20*
* *Free Breakfast, Lunch, and Dinner* *22*
* *A Tale of Two Social Groups* *23*
* *Bulls and Bears—Do's and Don'ts* *27*
* *Big Bucks! Big Cars! Big Houses!* *28*
* *Inherently Inept* *30*

CHAPTER 3   Auld Lang Syne 33

- *Patriotism—Memoirs of WWII and Our Freedoms* *33*
- *Patriotism! Today and Yesterday* *36*
- *Semper Fi! Hey Joe—Say It Isn't So!* *38*
- *Dogs: Precious Poodles, Mutts, and Special Breeds* *39*
- *Movies, Past and Present* *40*
- *Motoring, Before and After the Interstate* *41*
- *Survival Tactics in Northern Wisconsin* *43*
- *Whatever Happened to Romance?* *46*

CHAPTER 4   The Blithe Spirit 49

- *People Have Their Fun In Many Strange Ways* *49*
- *The Baseball Sage, Joe Six Pack* *50*
- *The Good, the Bad, and the Ugly in Baseball* *51*
- *Ya Gotta Be a Football Hero* *53*
- *Fanciful Flights of Fantasy* *55*

CHAPTER 5   Land of Enchantment 57

- *Florida—Land of Sunshine, Bugs, Thunderstorms and Old Timers* *57*
- *Florida's Dumb Stuff—It's Outrageous!* *58*
- *Spin Doctors and Developers Exacerbating Florida's Environmental Concerns* *59*
- *The Calamity of Negligence* *60*
- *I Need a Vacation—You Pick Up the Tab!* *63*
- *Disgruntled Employees, Totin Guns* *65*
- *Hang In There, You Old Buzzards* *66*

CHAPTER 6   Bewitched, Bothered and Bewildered 69

- *Only in America* *69*
- *Perfidy* *70*
- *Laws For Them and Laws For Us* *72*
- *Inquiring Minds Need to Know* *73*
- *Dr. Saxpot, It's Revolting!* *75*
- *Don't Breathe, It Could Be Hazardous to Your Health* *77*

CHAPTER 7   Turkeys, Eagles and Endangered Species 79

•   *Presidents Past and Present* *79*

CHAPTER 8   Stand Up and Cheer! 85

•   *An Essay on the Positive.* *85*

•   *Tree Woman Gave Us a Heroic Lesson.* *86*

•   *Two Heroes in our Midst.* *87*

•   *Something To Cherish.* *88*

•   *A Time for Reflection* *90*

In Summary 95

Acknowledgments

My first attempt at writing a book, namely this series of essays, was prompted by two sources. My wife Lorraine, who suggested I needed a hobby besides fishing. Friends, kinfolk, and my peers, many of whom are World War II veterans, also encouraged me to pursue this endeavor. Much of this was evoked by telephone calls and letters from people eliciting a favorable response to my letters to the editor, published in our local newspaper. The context of many of these letters appears in these essays.

My thanks are extended to my sister, Jane and my nephew, Tom and his wife, Susan for their encouragement to choose this course, a series of essays for publication.

To my son-in-law, Bill Maloney, I wish to express thanks for his creative contributions. We have enjoyed his inspirational poems in commemoration of Lorraine and Chuck's birthday and our 54th wedding anniversary.

To grandson, Ryan Salm and his wife, Mary for their letter of thanks to Grandma and Grandpa, which I felt was appropriate to the theme of Chapter 6.

I especially want to express my gratitude to my son, Kurt and his wife, Marsha for their efforts to have this manuscript typed on their computer for final analysis and final draft.

Since I have no formal schooling or training as a writer, I have no illusions of what acceptance may become of this effort. The motivating factor is in the hope that some publisher will find it worthwhile enough for an ordinary citizen to express his views about wrongs in our society that should be made right.

The validation of anything less than honorable human conduct by our leaders and citizenry can only result in our nation following in the path of the Roman Empire.

Participate, fellow Americans. Do not be content with *My Country, Right or Wrong*. Rather, *If My Country is Wrong, Make it Right!* Future generations depend on us doing the right thing.

Prologue

Tom Brokaw wrote a best seller, *The Greatest Generation.* Since I was born in Chicago on a blustery November day in 1924, that qualifies me as a member of that august generation. While I acknowledge our contribution to our country was honorable, I do believe that the generation of our founding fathers was truly "the greatest generation".

In the entryway of my home I have a framed copy of The Declaration of Independence. If ever an assembly of men were representative of a generation that deserves the esteem of succeeding generations, it is all of those during the Revolution that proclaimed themselves American. That document is a constant reminder to me of the sacrifice and challenges those first Americans faced.

When Thomas Jefferson drafted that venerable document, the Declaration of Independence became a reality on July 4, 1776. The freedoms we Americans have today did not come cheap. Those colonials shed blood for eight more years before final victory until we became "The United States of America". The colonials were now Americans.

In less than 30 years, our newly won freedoms were again in jeopardy. When Francis Scott Key saw that banner still waving over Fort McHenry on that September morning almost two centuries ago, he was inspired to write the verses that would become our national anthem.

In subsequent years, until the present date, wars have been fought, Americans gave their all, and families sacrificed to retain our freedoms. To reflect on the aforementioned has inspired me to use these freedoms and the liberty to express my views in this book of essays.

What is the point of this book? Why do I do this? Am I beating a dead horse? I write because countless patriots granted me this privilege through their sacrifice. No intolerant issue can be made right through silence and apathy. Many politicians will not do the right thing if it jeopardizes their careers, until their constituents apply enough heat.

Freedom can be a two-edged sword. We have institutions out there using their power and influence to the detriment of others. There are many issues that require vigilance by the average citizen. Many of our representatives in Washington take their careers for granted. A non-complacent citizenry could reverse this trend.

I love our rocks and rills, our purple mountain majesties and this sweet land of liberty. If I can redress what I consider an injustice upon my country or citizenry by the power of my pen, I will make that attempt. To be reticent would be to ignore what our flag stands for."

The themes of my writings are the viewpoint of a retiree and a veteran of World War II, who in the twilight years of my life, has made a decision to see if a non-celebrity can censure our culture and society in actions I believe to be detrimental to our nation.

Since my education is limited to that of a high school graduate, there will be no profound, deep intellectual prophecies concerning our nation's destiny. What you will read is the essence of my observations and dialogue with my peers who usually share my concerns.

I am a second generation American of German and French ancestry. American English was spoken in our home. No reference was ever broached to claim any bond to what was, at that time, described as "the Old Country". We, (Mom, Dad, my brothers and sisters), were as American as apple pie. The profound change in many Americans' morals and behavior that I have witnessed in my life is my fundamental concern. I perceive that these cultural changes will denigrate our country's future and the lives of succeeding generations.

There is no way to equate our country's immigration history beginning with the Revolutionary War and periods in our history of sacrifice and challenge, to the multitude of ungrateful newcomers to our shores. These ingrates demand their rights, profess their cultural superiority and refuse to assimilate into the great melting pot of the United States of America. To exacerbate matters, our pandering politicians, ever watchful to recruit new and unsophisticated voting blocks, are always willing to abide by their demands. This is one example of many unconscionable acts that make me as **mad as Hell!**

Like many Americans, my attitude toward politicians is generally negative. However bleak and pessimistic one becomes when we reflect on our perception of politicians, we must conclude that there must be some who are honorable and possess some manner of integrity. Otherwise, there is no hope. They are our elected officials and they are here to stay until we awaken from our complacency and vote them out of office. Our inevitable fate lies in our success in discovering and anointing the few good guys with some gray matter between their ears.

My dissent continues in many aspects of our society and culture, so bear with a grouchy old timer as I attempt to disprove the notion that we are a highly developed species. There are so many instances of eccentric behavior in our society that I do not find it difficult to depict our various character flaws. It makes one reflect on the theory that we humans utilize only a small part of our brains.

To the Reader

The following essays that comprise the various topics of this book were started in June of 2000. I took a hiatus of eleven months for personal reasons. Since then the tragedy of the events of September 11, 2001 traumatized our nation and galvanized our resolve to confront and wage war against the evil of the people who use terror as a means to an end. In this case, their goal seems to be the destruction of America by whatever means possible and however long it takes.

Not since December 7th, 1941, have the American people rallied around our President in our determination to exterminate the insidious forces allied to destroy us. This is a far different conflict than the war we faced against the Axis nations during WWII.

We now must confront a faceless opponent willing to sacrifice his or her life to inflict death and injury to innocent people to justify his or her unrestrained hatred of our culture and way of life.

The big question is, "How do we fight, how do we confront, and how do we defend against such a foe?"

The initial confrontational response was to go after the "big guy", Osama Bin Laden and his legions of miscreants.

Afghanistan was the military target to focus on as this was a known terrorist training ground and Osama's hideout. Our military has achieved a great accomplishment in destroying a huge cache of weapons and supplies. Many people in that region being trained as terrorists have been either captured or killed.

From all accounts, this is just the beginning of a long drawn out conflict with uncompromising zealots. The natural inclination after the citizenry of our country closed ranks with what seemed to be patriotic fervor was to have us take stock of our character flaws and foibles and shape up. This does not seem to be the case!

Greed seems to be an inherent fixture in the human persona, although in varying degrees from person to person. In our country, greed seems to take on a role as a driving force in our culture.

Our constitution was created by honorable men who lived in a time when honor and integrity were held in high esteem. We Americans take pride in our freedoms, as granted to us by the framers of our constitution. As a result of our freedoms, we are privy to the news media in all its forms presented to us on a daily basis. Many of the essays in this book were derived from that source, and my analysis there of. As the reader will note, the subjects are varied. Some are redundant, some serious, some tongue in cheek and satirical. Most are how I, "as a senior citizen" perceive the changes in my country that trouble and concern me.

Regarding my concerns on immigration and especially the multicultural aspect, I fully realize that we are a nation of people of varied ethnic ancestry. I went to school with kids of European and Asian lineage. Our neighborhood in Chicago was comprised of people of Irish, French, German, British, Polish, Italian, Bohemian, Swedish, and Armenian lineage.

We all had one thing in common. We all spoke English. We celebrated and understood the meaning of our national holidays. In school, we recited our pledge of allegiance.

This was part of *our* culture, *our* heritage; we were Americans. Now, in this day and age much of this is compromised by many of the people of other lands seeking refuge here and clinging to their language and culture and resisting any thought of assimilating in the American way of life and culture.

Every citizen in our country has the right to express their opinion by their actions, words, and deeds. If you wish to insist on not accepting the American culture and way of life, please take advantage of the freedom to get on a boat and go back to where you came from.

What better example of an ethnic group not of European ancestry that accepted the American lifestyle than the Nisei. "The Japanese

Americans who had no choice but to accept the fate of our government's decision to place them in detention camps during WWII."

Even though they had no choice but to accept this intrusion on their lives, their sons served with distinction in the military and proudly and honorably fought and many died in the European theater of war.

Although our country has conceded the error of having Japanese American families in detention and making reparations, it will always remain a blemish and reminder of our shortcomings.

Since I started this compilation of essays in June if 2000, I chose not to try and update any of them because the point I am trying to portray is that the foibles, nuttiness and nocuous behavior in our society never seems to diminish. In fact, it seems to flourish in our land.

At this point, I must forewarn you, gentle reader, of a bit of terminology that you may not have previously encountered. Several years ago a radio sportscaster on WJNO in West Palm Beach, Florida, was fond of using the term, *boobus Americanus* to describe the typical Joe Sixpack, the mindless sports addict who would endorse anything, no matter how outrageous, that would surface in professional sports. This deplorable creature would support, financially and morally, any shenanigan imaginable foisted on the general public by team owners and players. I took the liberty of expanding the term to include any of the multitudes of our countrymen and women who seem to be incapable of exercising critical thinking, personal responsibility and initiative. In short, I am including the people—you know who they are—who function with brain power just slightly above that of a **cabbage**.

Terrorism and the Challenge We Face

Lorraine and I were vacationing with friends in Ste-Anne De-Beaupre in Quebec, Canada on September 11, 2001. As I sipped coffee, I turned the TV on. My friend, Charles Koenig and I turned our attention to the news as we saw The World Trade Center ablaze from an apparent aircraft crashing into it. We watched in disbelief as another commercial jet slammed into and through the second tower.

Our thoughts and dialogue were a maelstrom of sadness, concern, rage and wonderment as we sat transfixed by the horror of the event we had just witnessed. We knew at once terrorism had struck our homeland.

This was the second day of a one-week vacation we had planned with our friends, Charles and Estelle Koenig from Concord, New Hampshire. We made the best of our vacation, but our TV was in use far more than we anticipated as the subsequent events enfolded on the news coverage. Much of our conversation was a result of the horrific event and how our country would react and cope with a tragedy of such magnitude. We pondered how our lives would be affected and how much determination we must summon to prevail against this tyrannical force we must confront.

Sunday, September 16th was the day of our departure from Canada, and we wondered how long it would take to cross the border. Surely vigilance would be the order of the day. No so! We breezed through with a cursory inspection. It gives one pause to reflect on how open our borders are. Since witnessing the inhuman brutality of such an evil act, it was difficult to comprehend the fact that security was so lax.

This tragedy has befallen our country, and the resolve of Americans to unite was exemplified by the determination and courage of the rescuers pulling victims to safety even as some of them succumbed to the dangers involved in their efforts. I found myself trying to hold back tears as I watched their valiant efforts continue as they ignored their fatigue.

The strength of our people is about to come face to face with much more than the display of our beloved flag. We have the wisdom and the courage to defend our country against any transgressor. The years that have gone by have bestowed on us a value system based on want and an extravagant lifestyle, replete with displays of selfishness and greed. The big question is—can we change 180 degrees to support our country's needs for a prolonged conflict with fanatics determined to break our will?

1

Doctrine of Confusion

SENIOR CITIZENS, HOW SWEET IT IS

Most of us *old timers* have lived not in just one, but more than likely several houses since we first experienced that wonderful place called home. As toddlers we knew that whatever trauma came our way comfort was close by. We became aware that Mom and Dad were there to not only comfort, but to care and provide for our needs. As we left the security blanket that had been provided for us, we began to realize that life is not always, "just a bowl of cherries". In the process, we began to think about just how capable are we, to cope with whatever life has in store for us.

We discovered ourselves, and others, some we admired, some we did not. We had been dealt some of the displeasure and distress that goes with life. We also had our magic moments that are stored in our memory bank.

For the most part, we had control over our abode. We could decorate and furnish it to suit our desires consistent to what we could afford. We could live in an urban area, the suburbs, or out in the countryside. In short, we had control over where and how we managed our needs, in home sweet home.

Now, for the not so sweet part! No matter where we choose to locate "our home", we are losing control. Many of my essays will either directly or indirectly reflect the nuances that are diminishing our quality of life. Our homeland is changing rapidly to our detriment. The basic cause is unrestrained immigration, legal and illegal. With the full knowledge that this topic is not politically correct and one could be labeled a racist, I believe anyone with a modicum of awareness must realize that breathing space and tranquillity are becoming a rare and evasive feature in our country.

As a senior citizen who has just recently had the honor of becoming a great-grandpa, my concerns are not so much for my generation, but for the little guy who just arrived on the scene. The doctrine of diversity foisted upon us from our national leaders, continuing unabated can only lead to chaos for future generations.

THE CASE FOR CYNICISM

The world has turned to brutish beasts and men have lost their reason!

I do not recall where I read that phrase, but it most likely is from one of the renowned English dramatists or poets, but it surely personifies the psychosis that seems to pervade what passes for civilization today.

If an alien from another planet were to observe human kinds' activities on a global scale, they most surely would concur that lunacy on planet earth is rampant.

The persistent violence that takes place, scattered across planet earth in the form of acts of war, terrorism, and assorted mayhem gives one pause to reflect on the fact that much of mankind's mental derangement is precipitated by religious intolerance.

Reverence for a superhuman power is the cornerstone for most religions. What happened to the reverence for human life?

If history is to be our guide, religious countries were never squeamish whenever the need arose to pursue violence on a grand scale, and zap those other non-believers or that other country that's throwing its weight around.

It makes one wonder how things would pan out if we were all heathens?

But that is beyond my reasoning abilities, so let's just concentrate on the notorious lack of reason in our own country that spawns so much cynicism among the citizenry.

Instances of dementia abound in our country when we consider the doctrine that we are taught in school and in church that life is precious. When the hue and cry of the "right to bear arms," rings across the land by the NRA and the *bubbas* in their ranks join the chorus, many of our congressional wimps prostrate themselves in submission and reverence to the NRA hierarchy, or face the consequences of an end to their careers.

Any reasonable attempt to minimize the carnage of gun violence is viewed as an attempt to take away an NRA member's handgun, hunting rifle, or shotgun. As a consequence, the NRA challenges any and all sensible bills presented to the House and Senate. Therefore, the gun happy goons in our midst, who have no regard for human life, have free reign to pursue their profane deeds.

If the stupidity of granting legality to immigrants invading our country without documentation were not enough to get your hackles up, now we have the specter of known foreign fiends in our jails about to be released, courtesy of our Supreme Court. These evildoers made it to our shores knowing full well about our benevolence toward law-breakers. Their homeland governmental officials will not take them back.

Are you getting mad yet? Or are you just gonna whine and lament, what can I do? Think about it! When these goons are out on the street, it won't take them long to be totin' a shootin' iron. That's about 3,400 bad guys on the loose, free to pursue whatever their criminal minds can conceive of.

Ancient Greek philosophers believed that self-control was the only way to achieve virtue. Many of our elected officials are motivated by a responsible attitude in their functions as public servants. But far too many have **little or no self-control**, especially when they spend money lavishly and with little thought to the burden imposed on the public that they are supposed to serve.

The late United States Senator from Illinois, Everett M. Dirksen, coined a phrase: "A billion dollars here and a billion dollars there, and soon we are talking about serious money." That was in the 60's; his hey-day. Wasteful spending of taxpayers' money seems to be a way of life. If the information we are privy to by the media is even remotely accurate, the enormity of taxpayers' money that is squandered by our elected officials, and our bloated bureaucracy, is probably beyond the average citizen's comprehension.

Think of the vast amount of money needed to fund the last presidential campaign. The Texas cowpoke spent millions just to assure victory over John McCain in the primaries. McCain was outspent about 8 to 1, which assured W's victory in the primary. Millions more had to be added to W's coffers to assure victory over Gore, who amassed millions for his own campaign. Then consider how much blather we were all exposed to in negativism via mailings, newspapers, magazines, and TV. 75% of what passed for important issues was dreary banality on both sides.

If that doesn't justify some cynicism, try to imagine that there is an intellectual young lion or lioness out there burning with the desire to enter the political arena. He or she has all the qualities we yearn for in a public servant...honor, righteous conduct, and integrity, but little or no access to the large amount of finances required in our present sphere of political clout.

But the "power of money" can assure anyone, regardless of his or her mediocrity, the best chance of victory in today's political morass.

At this writing, we are witnessing what could reasonably be construed as a blasé attitude toward moral principles by a body of men and women who regard themselves as an august assemblage, by the consideration of the electorate who placed them there. They have the capacity to cause the resignation of one of their own, who flaunts the principles of honor and virtue, which they would like us to believe they all subscribe to. This lofty virtuous creed is in fact sadly lacking by many in their rank.

Also, we have a congressman in the news, as he is the focus in the investigation of a missing young woman, a congressional intern, and a member of his staff. He has demonstrated a shameless propensity of deceitful behavior by lying about this affair with this young woman and the manipulation of the power and executive privilege as a congressman. This attitude of chicanery has hindered the police investigation and the cause of considerable consternation for the parents of this young woman.

His only involvement may be a case of personal embarrassment, but the whole scenario smacks of the special privileges granted to those who have, "the power of rank", and consider themselves elitists.

There is something terribly wrong in our country when honor and virtue are invalidated by the people who we expect to uphold the traditions upon which our country was founded.

The aforementioned examples point out a lack of prudence in the legislative and judiciary branches of government resulting in a lower standard of leadership. With no apparent challenge to this dubious conduct on the part of so many in command of our "ship of state", why would anyone be dismayed when college and professional athletes commit crimes such as rape, drunkenness and various sorts of mayhem, while their coaches validate their behavior so their team will not lose its status? We see many examples of Hollywood celebrities and rap artists held in high esteem, despite their low moral standards and abhorrent behavior.

Maybe the violence, madness, lack of leadership, rudeness, poor judgment, and abhorrent behavior is just a sign of the times and we will all just have to get used to it.

Maybe so. But count me out!

WHEN WE GO TO THE POLLS, CONSIDER HOW WE LOOK TO THE OUTSIDE WORLD

The recent presidential election with a lackluster candidate from Tennessee, and the man from Texas, deviated somewhat from the norm. To begin with, Presidential elections require financial contributions to beguile the electorate. Consider the obscene excess of financial contributions by the special interest groups funding both parties and their respective candidates. Pandering and a doctrine of perfidious allegations that had no equal that I know of highlighted this campaign.

"For all the qualified voters in our great land who tried to analyze and sort out the propaganda and the mother lode of trivia, we cast our ballots without enthusiasm, hoping we made the right choice under the circumstances. But the reality of presidential elections is the fact that we also have the party affiliation group who will vote as blind sheep no matter who is on their ticket. Last but not least, we have the *boobus Americanus* horde. If they choose to vote, he will be a regular guy or better looking; maybe he has a nice smile. Or it might be just one issue and the rest are not considered. For instance, the NRA mob—if he fondles his semi-automatic rifle, he's their guy."

Now as a result of our ambivalence and the ensuing trauma that we wrought upon our nation, we were under scrutiny by other nations. Never before in our history has the outcome of a presidential election been so close with two apparent lightweights for the American people to consider leading our nation. What with allegations of voter fraud, hanging chads, missing ballots, etc., etc., we have been judged as lacking in refinement and sophistication, especially by European countries, whose social graces are above reproach. ***Oh, yeah!*** But let us not despair—we can always feel confident that the British are goofier than we are.

AN AFFRONT TO DECENCY

The pervasive problem of child abuse in our country is a scandal fast becoming a crisis escalating in the annulment of morals. The Catholic Church in America, although beset by pedophile priests and accounts of sexual abuse, are by no means alone in this descent into immoral conduct. It cannot be denied that our country is obsessed with sex. By our country, I mean our culture! Our institutions, art, behavior patterns, in short our society is a breeding ground for perverts to crawl out of their *hidey holes* because sex in all of its forms permeates our social structure. As a consequence, there is no need to restrain what we once considered loose or licentious.

We are all aware of our new modern age in entertainment today. Just about every medium in our current mode of pleasurable pursuits has a good share of sex and violence for our perusal. The tragic part of this depraved scenario is where greed makes its presence known. Now the perverts come on the scene to beguile the immature.

The putrefaction of what passes for music among rap and rock groups today seems to mesmerize young people and take full advantage of the decadence that exists in our society and prosper. This mode of communication with our young and immature and the use of technology, to wit, the Internet, are some of the means for these *scum bags* to perpetuate the evil of luring young people to be participants in their depravity.

(Corporate America is no exception in this exploitation of our obsession with sex. They know how to utilize innuendo in this regard to promote their products.)

These are examples of the human element in our society that is self-serving and devoid of moral standards and ethics. It is disheartening that with our nation embroiled in a war on terror and the military and citizenry united in a common purpose, it is of no concern to those in our land whose only goal is self-aggrandizement and avarice, regardless of the consequence of their greed.

THIS IS YOUR FBI

I remember it well, that pugnacious bulldog countenance. He held the reins as Director of the FBI from 1924 until his death in 1972. Throughout his reign, his mug was on display quite frequently in newspapers and magazines. Under his leadership, the FBI distinguished itself as an efficient organization in combating organized crime and apprehending a variety of scoundrels in our land.

J. Edgar Hoover and his intrepid lawmen didn't give the bad guys much breathing room, and he made them sweat. This no nonsense attitude toward bringing these rogues to justice was vividly portrayed on radio and on television programs. However, in the later years under his direction, he was the center of controversy by claims of civil right violations and conservative political views.

Now at this writing, as many of our government agencies descend into the morass of ineptitude, the FBI would better be portrayed as the Keystone Cops.

Operational blunders, investigational screw-ups regarding spying, and various sundry acts of deficient performance are another example of inexplicable incidents taking place as we ponder our future. Hundreds of guns and laptop computers are missing. Thousands of pages of key documents in the Oklahoma City bombing case were never released. The spying caper screw-ups regarding the Wen Ho Lee espionage case, and the Robert Hanssen spy escapade are difficult to imagine in the scope of their ineptness.

Consider the fact that the number of weapons lost, amount to nearly 450 handguns, rifles, and sub-machine guns that add to the untold numbers already in the hands of fiends in our gun happy land. The way things are going, I hope the new Director can at least find agents capable of tracking a fiend with mud on his shoes and snot in his beard as he scampers to his hideout.

IMMIGRATION AND THE IMPACT ON OUR ENVIRONMENT

Unless mankind's leadership is devoid of reason, the problems of global population growth must be addressed. The consequences of our leader's inertia will only exacerbate the environmental disorder and social problems facing our nation.

The problem facing our country is the fact that our planet has in excess of six-billion people and most of them want to come to the good old U.S.A. and our immigration policy, (if you want to call it that), seems to be: Sure—why not!

This muddle headed thinking has been our bane for years. Is there no end to providing refuge to emigres who have created cesspools of their prior habitat, now streaming to our shores in ever increasing numbers and then demanding rights and taxpayer funded entitlements upon arrival? The effect on our country is all too evident unless you have lived on another planet for the last fifty years.

Birthrates among Americans of European heritage, as well as the people of prosperous industrial nations are stable. But, this is offset by the crush of both legal and illegal immigration to such an extent it can only degrade our quality of life.

Environmental debasement, already a problem, looms more ominous on the horizon. Traffic jams, (already intolerable), can only get worse. Trying to cope with life in overcrowded cities will be the norm. Our legacy will be an ever increasing throng of humanity to the extent that other species will be crowded out of their diminishing natural habitat, and humankind will deal with an increase in crime, disease, violence, poverty, and the inevitable result of our environment becoming more defiled.

According to the Organization of Zero Population Growth, population growth in every industrial country except the United States is decreasing. Immigration and children born to recent immigrants are fueling population growth.

We desperately need a moratorium on immigration!

JOE COLLEGE!—AND BETTY CO-ED, TOO!

Yes, there is no doubt about it. We have some gifted students in our colleges and universities. But, we seem to have a plethora of those in the *Boobus Americanus* category. Some seem to have just escaped from the sedimentary deposits of the **Pleistocene Era.**

How the Hell did they get in? Don't they have to meet some rudimentary requirements before they gain access to those hallowed halls of learning? Certainly they must know that the Berlin Wall does not separate China. What mental cretin told them that Harry Truman was a general in the Revolutionary War? How about Sandra Day O'Connor? These offspring of the Baby Boomer potheads think she was the first woman in space! These are examples of the answers some of our nation's brilliant college students gave when quizzed by TV talk show hosts on campus.

Hey dudes! Are we not the greatest? You betcha! We have the greatest number of dummies in our institutions of higher learning going out **dumber** than when they went in. It's not funny any more. Stop the exposés of these pinheads! It's humiliating for the whole world to know we have so many boneheads in our universities while we still proclaim ourselves to be *the greatest nation in the history of civilization.* Professor Kingsfield (played by the late John Houseman in the movie, *Paper Chase*) was prophetic in his pronouncement of his first year law students as *young skulls full of **mush.***

I subscribe to several magazines and read the daily newspaper. On more than a few occasions, I have read articles critical of our educational system. They have alluded to numerous ills:

• outdated and factually incorrect textbooks

• inept teachers

- do-little administrators

- overcrowded classrooms

- rowdy students

- lack of discipline

- lack of funds in the face of never ending property tax increases

The list goes on. In short, there has been a lot of *hot air* about improving our public schools' ability to impart knowledge, but we still grant diplomas to semi-literates. At this writing, President Bush finally recognizes the fact that a proper education requires a voucher to attend a private school. And so, the sad saga continues. Somehow we manage to supply our schools of higher learning with unmotivated laggards studying **something.**

Joe College is now about to graduate *summa cum laude* but he is required to give a correct answer to this last oral final exam question to the disinterested and enfeebled (but, **tenured**, mind you) Professor Zempft.

> Professor Zempft: "Joe, what is a *calorie?*"
> Joe (proudly): "Somethin' ya eat!"
> Professor Zempft: "What, Joe? Speak up!"
> Joe (with gusto): "**Somethin' ya eat!**"
> Professor Zempft: "That's right—**a unit of heat!**"

That was several years ago. Joe has capitalized on his academic prowess and is now a tenure track professor at **Neanderthal University**.

GUN NUTS, THE NRA & POLITICIANS

Plagues of various descriptions have been a destructive force since time immemorial. A locust plague descended on Brigham Young's settlement in Utah about 150 years ago. Gulls seemed to appear out of nowhere and devoured the locusts. Some imply that divine intervention had a hand in this apparently miraculous event.

It would seem that we need an event of divine intervention to stem the tide of gun violence in our nation. The gutless performance by so many Republicans and some Democrats in the House and Senate has added credence to my belief that most of them are no more than self serving sheep, just like the Billy Bob's who are brainwashed by the N.R.A. hierarchy.

Guns in America are a plague! This is but one example of why so many citizens feel contempt for so many of our spineless, dishonorable politicians. I am afraid we have reached a new low when it seems we have representatives who cannot summon up enough courage to pass a bill to make it more difficult for kids and wackos to get guns.

There was a time when the N.R.A. was a credible institution. They seem to have degenerated into a cadre of zealots. Their agenda seems to be: We want more guns, more ammo, and the hell with the rest of society. They have become a powerful cult with deep pockets, offerings supplied by their *bubbas*.

With the exception of one Roman Catholic priest, who wrote an article lambasting the evils of the N.R.A. and the gutless legislators who are under the dominion of The Big Honcho and his sidekick, there seems to be a profound silence by the clergy on this issue, despite the fact that many denominations have adopted resolutions favoring gun controls.

It is quite evident that legislators are not the only ones subjugated by the N.R.A.

THE DEMISE OF REASON

As World War II drew to a close, everyone who experienced the trauma wrought by that conflict embraced a very popular song (do you remember it, folks?): *There will be love and laughter and peace ever after, tomorrow, just you wait and see.*

All of us in that generation, civilians and military, could not imagine humankind not following that dream after two world wars in our century put a closure on the insanity of war.

Since that time, we have had the Korean War, Vietnam War, Gulf War, skirmishes and conflicts, and now the War on Terror, which might last until Hell freezes over.

Consider for a moment, *Lunitus Floridus*, that dreaded mental degeneration known to particularly plague Floridians, now seems to have engulfed the entire nation. To wit, what we have been privy to in the media in recent days:

- The expense involved, *estimated in the millions*, that illegal immigrants pass on to the taxpayer for medical care they receive in our hospitals and clinics.

- A big-rig truck blasts through a stop sign at 70 mph, slamming into a school bus, injuring the driver, 15 school children and the bus driver. The truck driver had a suspended license and five prior convictions for various violations.

- Menorah Gardens, under the auspices of the world's largest burial provider, violated a sacred trust by mistreating the dead and deceiving their families and covering up their errors.

- A crematorium not in use for years; bodies thought to be cremated found scattered in the woods, some piled up like cord wood. Authorities draining a nearby lake searching for more remains. Over 300 bodies discovered.

- Bail granted to an Iranian businessman (a resident alien) found toting a gun between flights to Miami.

- A judge in Massachusetts granting probation to a man convicted of raping a 14 year old girl.

- The Roman Catholic Church reeling from disclosures of a Cardinal in Boston keeping secret a priest with a history of child molestation and the ensuing disclosure of pedophilia problems with priests elsewhere in the U.S.

I'm convinced each succeeding day will bring us more news of various forms of dementia that seem to plague our fair land. Until then, folks, just do your own thing. Nobody's minding the store!

THE CALAMITY OF NEGLIGENCE

I don't know what kind of people work for Florida's *Department of Children and Families*. They certainly seem to be beset by inefficient employees. To say they are lax in attending to duty is an understatement, but to say criminal intent is involved is too strong. Somewhere in between lies a real and disturbing problem.

I have made a point of stating that most of us are not privy to the knowledge that people in power possess. We read and hear the news, but what goes on behind the curtain, we will never know.

The case of 5 year old Riyla Wilson is consistent with the deplorable state of the indolent disposition of the DFC's personnel. Little Rilya Wilson disappeared from state care 15 months before she was reported missing. As of this date, June 24, 2002, according to an article in *The Ledger*, a newspaper serving Polk County, Florida, 1237 children under state care cannot be located. How's that for a casual attitude regarding child welfare?

If that's not enough to raise your hackles, maybe this will! The following are excerpts from *The Ledger*, dated June 23, 2002:

Five years ago, the Roe children, five brothers and their sister emerged battered but alive from the grasp of state approved Foster parents who locked them in a room, beat them regularly and fed them a diet of *Nyquil* and cereal soaked in *Kool-Aid*. The following excerpt describes what these 6 children endured at the hands of Jackie and

John Lynch, the Foster parents. The children's ages are: Jesse, 15; twins Jordan and Joseph, 14; Toby, 12: and Twins Suzanna and Robbie, 9.

Except for beatings, meager feedings, and erratic days at school, the children rarely left the small room that made up their world from 1990 to 1997.

Occasionally, Jordan or Joseph would slip out of the locked room through a window near the top of the door and rummage for food to bring back to the others. Thjey were caught and beaten, and the Lynches covered the opening with wire.

After attorney Howard Talenfeld filed a suit on behalf of the Roe children against DCF in 1999, documents surfaced that indicate the agency had evidence that the Lynch home was not a safe place for children.

Records showed that Jackie Lynch's daughter from a prior marriage was removed from her care in 1987 for sexual and emotional abuse. Frank Lynch had an arrest record for obstruction of justice and owed $16,000 in child support payments to his own biological children. And as a teenager living with the young Roes, Michael Lynch was arrested after he videotaped himself having sex with a 14 year old girl.

The children said Michael beat them and often shoved Joseph or Jordan inside a plastic crate, taped it shut and threw it in the pool as the boy struggled for air.

"I used to think—I'm going to die," said Jordan.

Talenfeld argued that the children's constitutional right to safety had been violated by the DCF.

"It's impossible for me to comprehend that anyone could torture these six beautiful children," said Talenfeld.

The Lynches paid a $140 fine and now live in Alabama.

All six if the Roe siblings agree they survived the ordeal by looking out for one another.

"We stuck together," said Jordan. "We depended on Jesse. He kept track of us, kept us in line."

"I didn't know I had that responsibility," said Jesse, 15. "I didn't know what a normal life was."

The basketball player is learning to drive and wants to be a Navy Seal.

Since becoming part of the Rodrigues family, the children go to school and spend time camping, boating, and eating chili cheese dogs. Memories of the Lynch years linger, but they are safely shared among family. I've tried to put everything behind me," says Jesse. "There's a lot more to do than be stuck in a room."

They are now in the care of Kathy and Rod Rodrigues who left a 21 year career to become a full time Foster parent.

To fathom the depths of Florida's idiosyncrasies is challenging, to say the least. Here's another article by Brian Bandell of the Associated Press for you, dear reader to ponder the vapid state of affairs here in *Wonderland.*

Bush: No Grand Jury for Missing Children

MIAMI—Gov. Jeb Bush has refused to create a statewide grand jury to investigate the 1,237 children under state care who can't be located.

The Department of Children & Families has classified most of these children as either runaways, out-of-state or taken from their homes by either by a family or relative. None of them were visited in May.

State Rep. Frederica Wilson, D-Miami said the department need to account for these children to make sure thy haven't gone missing like 5-year old Rilya Wilson, who disappeared from state care 15 months before she was reported missing.

She said the proposal is supported by the Florida Black Caucus and the other members of the state government.

Wilson sent several letters to Bush and called his office asking to meet with him and discuss a grand jury. She said she didn't receive a response.

At a fund-raiser Saturday, Bush said he was aware of her requests, but denied them choosing to stick with the recommendations of a Blue Ribbon Panel that he appointed to investigate the DCF.

"We've taken the recommendations of the Blue Ribbon Panel and we're moving on to improve the system," Bush said.

Wilson said the panel's recommendations were already included in the DCF's guidelines for years, but they've never been followed. A grand jury would be more effective, she said, because it could subpoena people to testify.

Bush downplayed the number of children the DCF hasn't visited and said that no investigation is needed.

Add to this, the day-by-day articles that we who reside here, read in our local blurb. Most of the articles elicit the usual response—*unbelievable*! After living in Florida for a while, or just about anywhere else, for that matter, we quickly change to, "Yeah, I can believe that." Nothing surprises us any more.

Just recently a Muslim woman obtained a driver's license in which the photo showed her with her head covering with only her eyes visible to anyone attempting to verify her identity. The *goofus* who granted her the license in this manner was informed that it was a mistake making it invalid. Now the Driver's License Bureau is being sued by this woman on the grounds of denying her religious freedom.

Florida seems to be surpassing California in outlandish behavior in just about all aspects of human endeavor. My guess is that it is because we have a *welcome mat* that proclaims:

Give me your lethargic,
Give me your bizarre,
Give me your unlawful.

That's how I read it. Help!

We don't need this cornucopia!

2

To Have or Have Not

THE RICH, THE ULTRA-RICH, THE HUNGRY AND THE HURTING

Our nation is experiencing hard times! The stock market is in the throes of a descent bordering on a recession. Our portfolios are causing us terrible anguish. People are being laid off in droves. There is no consumer confidence. The sky is falling!

When I sally forth and hit the road, I see two SUV's to every one sedan, and most sedans are luxury or gas-guzzlers. The shopping malls seem to have generous supplies of folks extracting credit cards from their wallets and purses. Automobile showrooms are full of people kicking tires. Watering holes and restaurants are humming with activity.

I find hard times hard to find when I stray from my abode. When I go to the dentist, he does not have any compassion for my financial distress when he tells me each of the two crowns I need are going to cost $900.00 apiece.

Boats in Florida are always in Vogue. Don't want no small boats! Taxes on boats are big. Boats are expensive. Doesn't matter, just dig deeper into that wallet or grab the credit card to postpone the pain. Here on the Treasure Coast of Florida, the marinas are very busy. Many are building additions to accommodate demand for storage and showroom space for big boats.

Homebuilders and developers are outdoing each other in building big homes, not those dinky little 2,000 square foot pads for $200,000 to $300,000. Do you want a condo on the beach with an ocean view? A cheap one goes for about $500,000.

How about those greedy corporate executives and the greedier CEO's? What if their portfolios took a hit? So what if the chief lost 35%? He is down to only $62,000,000 now. We will just to have to cut the dividends on our floundering company and boost his salary more in stock options. When he retires, he wants that exclusive country club pad on the oceanfront and a ranch in Montana for the summer months. Nothing really pretentious, only about $15,000,000 for a modest cottage on the beach and $7,000,000 for a nice hacienda on that 2,600 acres he acquired when he had lunch with Senator Blowhard from Montana.

Well, that's life at gold and diamond intersection. But what about the folks toughing it out on deprivation row? I know they're out there because after you have contributed to several charities that you think are *legit*, you're on the list.

So here I am, caught in the middle, torn between salvaging my bleeding portfolio, and to whom, and how many times should I say yes to the never ending charities reminding me that 84% of our populous is either homeless, destitute, or starving.

I am sure that there are people in our land of plenty, who do not have plenty, who are hurting and hungry. I wonder, though, how many people out there are accepting handouts and charity and are overweight, wearing golden chains and earrings. The meek might inherit the Earth, but the carnivores are in control in this world.

IT'S GREAT TO HAVE CHARISMA

"Boy, that guy is really cool!"

"He sure is. It's known as *charisma*, my boy."

"Are you a reporter?"

"Yes, for a national magazine—my first assignment."

"Recent grad with a degree in journalism?"

"Yes."

"What about you. What are you here for?"

"I'm just a spectator. I like his speeches. What's your name, kid?"

"Dave. What's your handle?"

"Just call me Lou."

"They're calling him the *Comeback Kid*. He's got a big following in the good old USA and they love him in France and England, too."

"Yes, I know. That's what's so amazing. Everyone knows he's a liar and a cheat. In short, completely dishonorable, yet so many people revere him."

"Ah, but he has *charisma*!"

"You know, Lou, we just had a presidential election and we had two dullards with no charisma or inspirational wizardry and yet, they beat out all of their opponents in the primaries. They went neck and neck down to the finish."

"Yes, that's true, but they had the next best thing going for them—access to **lots of money.** Big bucks! Money is power, kid."

"For a reporter, kid, you're kind of naïve."

"Well, smart guy, what's your formula for success? You look sophisticated. You're fashionably dressed and prosperous."

"First you must assess the human condition, then take full advantage of it."

"And, in your humble opinion, what would that be?"

"**Greed!** Think about it, kid. Throw in charisma and guile and there is no limit to what you can accomplish. Look at all those fools out there, entranced by his charismatic persona. He's playing on their weaknesses."

"Which are?"

"Their tolerance for his immoral principles; they cannot differentiate between right and wrong. They are sanctioning everything he stands for. They want to know how they can get what he's got. Many of them lost their asses now that the market is in the tank. They're pissed off. They want to know—where's mine?"

"Greed played a big part in building this country, kid. Without the railroad tycoons, bankers and the big industrialists that amassed fortunes by the exploitation of cheap labor, we would not be where we are today."

"Which is?"

"At a **crossroads**, kid!"

"Listen, Lou, I know a lot of people I admire that have charisma."

"Oh, who would that be?"

"Well, all those that volunteer for charities and help people in need. They all seem to have a special gift. I guess you could call it charisma, too. There are people in all walks of life that would fit that mold."

"Yeah, but they're *different*, kid."

"I gotta go, Lou. By the way, you will be in my story on this assignment, Lou. You're a classy guy. You have a certain flair. I guess you even possess a kind of charisma in your own right."

"Just for the record, Lou, what's your full name?"

"I only go by one name."

"How do you spell it?"

"**L-U-C-I-F-E-R**"

FREE BREAKFAST, LUNCH, AND DINNER

It's infuriating! Here I am standing in line at the checkout counter with about ten items my wife asked me to pick out and utilize the coupons to help in our cost cutting on groceries. My gripe is the couple in front of me in the checkout line. They are loaded down with groceries that you and I are paying for. If they were truly needy with circumstances beyond their control, I would have no beef.

This couple, however, did not seem to fit that criterion. I don't know what standard is used to determine who can use the *freeloaders card* that people use now in lieu of food stamps. Both had an assortment of jewelry decorating their lunch hooks. She also displayed what appeared to be golden earrings. He had a chain around his neck and a little doodad in his pierced ear, both objects looked like gold.

Since I do not do much of the grocery shopping, I am not cognizant of the ways freeloaders can justify their pilferage of our "tax payers" money. When I told my wife the story of what I had witnessed, the flash of "the card" signifying, go ahead, "It's on Uncle Sam", Her response was "I see it all the time." She qualified this by referring to the needs of people who do not abuse the system and have a legitimate right to be on welfare.

In subsequent conversations with friends, we heard the same refrain, "We see it all the time." I guess it's inherent in our culture. We seem to be generous to those among us who are indolent and know how to use the system to perpetuate their lifestyle.

At least that was my perception when I stood in line at the checkout counter and became enlightened. Now I am well aware of my peers theme, "We see it all the time."

It kind of makes you feel like you're between the "rock and the hard place," when you agonize over your Income Tax form and realize you're not going to get a refund. Ante up you suckers. Uncle Sam needs more of your hard-earned cash.

Forget about making improvements on your home, your reward for your industriousness will be an increase in your real estate tax.

A TALE OF TWO SOCIAL GROUPS

Elitism is defined as a sense of being part of a superior or privileged group, so you might say that an elitist is more enlightened, more intelligent, and refined. He or she is a visionary, so as a consequence of belonging to this elevated social status, these grand specimens of homosapiens should by right control our destiny.

But who in this great land are these privileged masters in command of our ship of state? Are they the descendants of old money or Ivy

League universities? Do they belong to the most exclusive clubs and disdain those who do not?

Who cares! The problem we have to contend with, (regardless of our social status), is that we have too many in positions of power that have this mindset. From the Supreme Court all the way down to Podunk County Court, many judges will fit this mold. How many bonehead rulings have been made by judges who have the inherent privilege of not being held accountable?

Steady, you peons, heah come dah judge. Everyone rises as his majesty makes his dramatic entry attired in his magnificent robe. Could these eminent legal scholars of the law be considered elitists? After all they are just lawyers who have been promoted.

Are our presidential aspirants and legislators elitists? Of course not! They are "good old boys or gals". They're folks, just like us. They shake our hands, they kiss our babies, and they make patriotic speeches. They assure us of great expectations. But now that they have attained their goal, they are in command. They have all the answers that the ordinary Americans out there could not possibly understand the challenges our nation faces. Many believe they now possess the wisdom and knowledge that marks them as elitists. **Baloney!** They are wannabe elitists who are ordinary folks, most of whom have university backgrounds. Some have served with distinction in our armed services. Some have distinguished themselves by avoiding the military. All have gained renown by periodically voting themselves hefty raises, magnificent retirement plans, and health benefits.

How about the Po Folks, the Bourgeoisie, the Middle Class? Yes, the other social group that contributes the lion's share of tax money to the general fund.

This is the fund that provides the congressmen and senators a retirement fund most of us could only dream about. They contribute nothing to this fund.

But we get cost of living adjustment on our social security benefits. Ah, be not dismayed fellow serfs. Our legislators know how to look after our best interests. As of this writing, 7/29/2001, in our local blurb, *The Stuart News* proclaims **Social Security Reform Bill Proposes Reductions in Guaranteed Benefits.** The authors of this congressional proposal are representatives Jim Kolbe, Republican from Arizona, and Charles Stenholm, Democrat from Texas:

> *Since the presidential campaign, Bush has promoted the benefits of allowing workers to invest part of their payroll taxes in stocks and bonds. But he has avoided specifying how he will pay for the transition to the investment accounts, or saying what other measures he will back to ensure that Social Security can pay promised benefits to the 76 million baby boomers after they retire.*
>
> *The two said personal accounts alone would not solve the problem. To pay for the accounts and to put the system on sound footing, they plan to propose reducing the guaranteed benefit, especially for middle and upper income workers, increasing the level of earnings subject to the Social Security payroll tax and reducing cost-of-living adjustments.*
>
> *The plan also would accelerate the schedule for raising the retirement age to 67 from 65, and it would reduce annual benefits further in line with any future increases in life expectancy.*
>
> *The plan also will divert some tax revenues from Medicare, worsening the already weak financial condition of that program.*
>
> *Kolbe and Stenholm said proceeds from the investment accounts would at least make up for cuts in the guaranteed benefit. Moreover, they said, the system would avert the certainty of even bigger benefit cuts and huge tax increases if nothing was done.*
>
> *To offset some of the proposal's painful measures, the plan would provide benefit increases to low-income workers and would match part of any money invested by people with low incomes in their personal accounts.*
>
> *But even with the sweeteners, Kolbe and Stenholm said they knew their plan would attract intense criticism. Stenholm said he and Kolbe were like canaries being sent into a mineshaft for Bush and other advocates of changing the system, putting themselves on the line to gauge what the two parties are willing and able to do.*
>
> *Most of the changes would be phased in so that they would not affect anyone now receiving retirement benefits or within a decade of retirement.*

Critics of Bush's approach said the Kolbe-Stenholm bill shows that the administration would find it nearly impossible to come up with a politically acceptable plan that included private accounts—at least without relying heavily on general tax revenues to pay part of the bill, a step the White House has made clear it is loath to take.

"The combination of the lack of general revenues and the diversion of financing into individual accounts creates unbearable pressure on the rest of the program," said Peter R. Orszag, a former Clinton administration economist and expert on Social Security.

Charles P. Blahous, staff director of the Bush commission, said the panel would look at every constructive proposal made by members of Congress or other people with an interest in the subject.

"The most important aspect of the Kolbe-Stenholm proposal is that it's a bipartisan collaboration, and we're trying to build a bipartisan atmosphere," Blahous said.

Social Security is taking in more through payroll taxes than it needs to pay benefits. But that situation will change rapidly starting in about 15 years as the bulk of Americans born from 1946 to 1964 move into retirement.

By 2016, under projections, Social Security will need to start drawing on its holdings of government bonds to pay benefits. By 2038, the bonds will be exhausted, leaving the system capable of paying only about 72 percent of promised benefits.

Most Republicans in Congress support the idea of private accounts, but they have been reluctant to back any plan requiring benefit cuts or tax increases. Most Democrats—Stenholm is an exception—oppose private accounts, saying they do nothing to solve the system's problems and introduce risk into what should be a guarantee against poverty in old age.

With the problem still years away, neither party has made a serious push so far to address the issue. Whether Bush has the clout to push a plan through Congress next year is the subject of much debate.

Kolbe and Stenholm have been pushing versions of their plan for several years but have generated little overt support in Congress. The significance of their bill lies less in its prospects for passage, which are slim, than in their willingness to prepare the public on Bush's behalf for the tough choices that were obscured when the issue was last aired, in the presidential campaign."

Sleep well tonight folks. ***Your future is in the hands of the elite!***

BULLS AND BEARS—DO'S AND DON'TS

Judgment day on Wall Street! It came in the mail today, in real big bold blue letters. And underneath in big black, but not bold, letters, the caption proclaimed:

This $5 trillion stock market bloodletting guarantees an economic upheaval of catastrophic proportions in 2001–2002. Here's what you must do immediately to preserve your wealth. I don't know what wealth he is referring to; the recent rampage by the Bear decimated my portfolio. And double and redouble your money with every new decline in stocks. This prophet, or profit, dear reader, is Martin D. Weiss, PhD, President, Safe Money Investor Service.

This guy is not just your everyday stock market analyst. He's a magician. He reminds us in no uncertain terms how the Bear tore our portfolio to shreds, but will show us how our shrunken assets can be quadrupled in the coming money panic. This is an urgent warning. Do not procrastinate.

Now wait a minute! No need to get sweaty palms, or a rapid heartbeat. The mailman also delivered Louis Rukeyser's consistently upbeat newsletter. It only took a brief scanning of the first page and the disquietude I endured by Dr. Weiss's forecast of the impending calamity, was soon replaced by an aura of complete calm.

On the front page, Mr. Rukeyser's Wall Street blurb, proclaimed in extremely large black letters, "Are technology stocks dead?" Somewhere between big and large, he proclaims, "My answer is Bull." And I want to tell you why…

Now is that comforting or what?

Hold it! Hold it! My wife just informed me that I overlooked Louis Rukeyser's Special Issue report on Louis Rukeyser's fund recommendations.

This time, in huge black letters, he tells me how to prevent my lousy mutual fund manager from running me into the poor house. Most of my portfolio consists of mutual funds. All of the mutual fund managers in charge of my investments were running *can't-miss* funds according to recommendations from mutual fund analysts. Guess what? The majority of my mutual funds have lost 30 to 50% percent or more in value.

Financial planners, stockbrokers, and investment companies in Florida target senior citizens by enticing you to a free lunch or dinner, to spin a yarn about investment strategies. These enticements come by mail, newspaper ads, and telemarketing. Their expertise will show you how to profit in the next bull market, or avoid the pitfalls in the next session of bloodletting. It all depends on who knows best, the optimists, or the guys pushing the panic button, so the average geezer, (myself included), sallies forth to these marvels of financial renown. After the seminar, the geezers get together and discover that the double talk we have been privy to, we already know, when we separate the wheat from the chaff.

What most of us have concluded is, that most people engaged in this endeavor of enlightenment, by hosting these seminars are doing so in good faith, but with the stock market in the tank at this writing, business is not too good. It is doubtful if anyone can predict where the stock market is headed with the world in a constant state of flux. Nevertheless, the assorted gurus out there conjure up diverse ways to drum up business.

BIG BUCKS! BIG CARS! BIG HOUSES!

Big is big in our country, don't want no small stuff. From time to time, we have an economic problem that manifests itself in an energy crunch. Conservation, frugality, saving? Not in my country. Abundance, extravagance, waste, ah that's our lifestyle.

Gimme that thing, that SUV that gets 10 mpg! How about that big camper that turns in automatically at every gas station? When the fuel costs spiral up, and the oil barons greed causes considerable anguish for motorists, the knee-jerk reaction is, why doesn't Detroit make smaller more efficient cars? We don't want small cars, we want big cars and cheap gas. Our economy is based on abundance, spacious, grandiose, and the waste perpetuated by our wanton behavior patterns. And don't forget big houses on big lots!

This quirk in our persona is evident in our consumptive way of life. One of the most apparent is the more than ample amounts of food we consume. Consider the ever increasing restaurants serving all you can eat brunches, buffet lunches, dinners, etc.

Then observe the proliferation of fat people, fatter people and human whales, as we waddle back and forth to add to our corpulence.

So we revel in our opulence and languish in our complacency. Elegance and extravagance in our society knows no bounds.

Sports figures, celebrities, and C.E.O.s have no constraint to their greed and for the most part, we admire them. Greed in our culture is no longer considered a deadly sin. It is pursued with wild abandon. The mood of our times is: *Where is mine?*

So where is this euphoria leading us? My perception is a false sense of security. Since our legislators are also lulled into the aforementioned state, they do not address many of our problems until they reach the crisis stage.

The following article was published in our local paper, with data provided by the organization of zero population growth. A child born in the United States will consume as much energy over a lifetime as three Japanese, six Mexicans, twelve Chinese, 33 Indians or 147 Bangladeshis.

If the kid becomes a fatso, which is very probable in our province of unrestrained want, and after the taunts endured in childhood, he or she will fit into our ever increasing obese social class.

INHERENTLY INEPT

The dumbing-down of educational standards seems to be generally accepted as factual in many of our schools. We have many high school graduates happily accepting their diplomas, who are marginally literate. Some colleges and universities offer Mickey Mouse courses to enable students to get the required credits to graduate.

For whatever reason, we seem to have an abundance of people in every business category that seem to be totally inadequate to their job description.

The following tale of woe is representative of situations that we encounter with more and more frequency. When a problem arises from a bill, statement, or almost any form of communications between a household and whatever business your dealing with, you must overcome the following barriers in order to point out a mistake on their part:

• You must deal with the recorded message and menu.

• After eternal hold, or a disconnect, you usually encounter person number one.

• You are transferred to another department, wrong department, or transferred again.

• Communication is difficult. The person barely speaks or understands English.

• After one to two frustrating hours on the phone, dealing with lazy and indifferent non-communicative people, you get the person who has been promoted to their highest level of incompetence—**supervisor.**

Now you must go through the whole procedure again. The supervisor will look into the matter and call you back. She is irritated by your persistence. You can tell by her voice.

After three days, there is no response. You call back. You ask to speak to her. You are on hold, as they try to locate her. She is on vacation. She will be back in two weeks. Can anyone else help you? Maybe Joe Blow, but he (wouldn't you know it?) is in a meeting. Seven days later, you receive a letter stating the error has been corrected. Your statement was mixed up with another account.

In discussions with my peers, I find that the situation just described is comparable to what many have had to cope with, and concur is quite a common trait in business today.

Most situations only take a few hours, or at the most, several days of phone calls to get resolved. Real bonafide *boobus Americanus* situations can try your sanity when it takes weeks or even months to end the madness of dealing with people having IQs of a cabbage.

It took us four months of dealing with people consumed with inertia, to resolve a problem regarding telephone bills sent to our Florida address from AT&T.

We left Illinois to our new home in Florida, and we followed the proper procedure required for a final billing and disconnect from AT&T when we sold our home in Illinois. After about four months in our Florida home, we began to receive bills from AT&T attributed to an Illinois address at which we never resided, but was being billed to us. The phone number we had in Illinois was now held by another party. We sent the bills back, stating that we no longer lived in Illinois. We requested that the bills be sent to owner or occupant of the aforementioned address in Illinois, who now had our previous Illinois telephone number. Our suggestion was seemingly ignored as the bills kept coming to us, while the other party got a free ride.

In desperation, we began making phone calls. After four months in a futile effort of talking to everyone at AT&T who could speak some level of understandable English, we eventually found a person who could actually *think* and had the capacity for rational thought. Our suggestion of calling the occupant or owner of the Illinois address was finally acted upon. The bills were never sent to the party who was using that particular telephone number. We finally breathed a sigh of relief and then promptly canceled our appointment with *the shrink*.

In the days and weeks following, articles in various newspapers and magazines in our local library were shedding some light on certain blue chip companies who were faring badly, while their CEO's were vacuuming in **big bucks**.

Can you guess who was in the top ten?

3

Auld Lang Syne

PATRIOTISM—MEMOIRS OF WWII AND OUR FREEDOMS

It's burned in my memory bank. I was seventeen when I stepped onto a bus, as I left my older sister and brother in-law's domicile to go home. I was greeted by the bus driver's exclamation, "The Japs bombed Pearl Harbor!" It was difficult to comprehend. I was aware of Japanese and American negotiations, but as for the context or reasons, it was all very vague in my mind.

At that time in my life, my thoughts and activities were pretty much consumed by schoolwork and school projects, baseball, and involvement with my peers. Although that sneak surprise attack took a heavy toll of American lives and destroyed much of our Navy and facilities at Pearl Harbor, it was the biggest mistake the Japanese could have made.

Things changed in America overnight. Our nation became galvanized as never before in our history. Germany, heady with their armies overrunning Europe declared war on us, as we declared war on Japan.

My cousin, eager to get at the Japs, joined the Marines. I wanted to follow suit. Mom and Dad said, "after you graduate from high school."

Five days after receiving my diploma, the mailman delivered a greeting card from the draft board. I chose the navy and boot camp at Great Lakes Naval Training Center in North Chicago, Illinois. I was among many thousands of boys and young men who found themselves shouldering arms in training camps from coast to coast. I never considered the fact that I could be a casualty in this worldwide conflict. I guess this is why young men are chosen to fight wars. This was a once in a lifetime adventure. After all, we were Americans. The Axis powers must be nuts if they thought they could beat us. Bravado was the order of the day. We soon became aware of the fact that the Japanese and Germans had their share of bravado also. They were tough disciplined adversaries.

That conflict lasted from 1939 to 1945 and involved civilian populations on an unprecedented scale. Military deaths probably amounted to some 17 million, but civilian deaths were undoubtedly much higher because of mass bombings of cities and the ensuing starvation, epidemics, massacres, and other war-related causes.

Nearly every major power in the world was involved, divided into two groups. The Allies consisted principally of Great Britain, the United States, the Soviet Union, and China. The Axis Powers were composed of Germay, Italy, and Japan.

My contribution began when I was assigned a tour of duty on a freighter as a signalman, a member of a U.S. Naval gun crew, which would join a convoy of ships delivering military personnel to the British Isles, and thence to Murmansk, Russia.

We were one of the more fortunate convoys on what was known as, "The Russian Run." The trip to Murmansk was uneventful. The trip back was not so lucky. Several ships sunk by stuka dive-bombers and floating mines off of the North Cape of Norway. The most harrowing incident was that of a storm which threatened to capsize our ship, due to shifting ballast in the hold. Lifeboat drills were curtailed. This was March and in those northern latitudes, hypothermia would take its toll in short order.

Next stop, Glasgow, Scotland to join a convoy to assemble for the next mission, our part in "Operation Overlord,' the Normandy invasion. Our group did not participate in the initial invasion. After several weeks of wondering if we would be victims of the buzz bombs finding their way in the vicinity of the Isle of Wight, our staging area, we finally headed for the Normandy coast, along with many other ships. Our cargo was more military personnel and supplies.

The beachheads had been established and our guys were pushing in. It was at a terrible cost. Soldiers that never made it to the beach were still being released from the deep, where they had drowned and were carried out by the ebb tide.

We watched in wonder as hour after hour allied bombers, wave after wave heading for targets in Germany. I remember a caption in a newspaper clipping sent to me from home,"The Dying Gladiator" depicting a German soldier about to receive, "The Coupe De Grace" That was to be their fate, as they stubbornly resisted in a lost cause.

When American and British troops set foot on German soil, the horror of the concentration camps they liberated were revealed. The Nazi regime that maintained the concentration camps forced Jews and many ethnic political prisoners, including some Germans into hard labor with minimal nutrition to perform their tasks. Those physically unable to work were exterminated. What they referred to as *The Final Solution* was total extermination of Jews.

I had no personal encounter with these atrocities, but in subsequent trips across the Channel, we carried GI's wounded or in need of R & R back to England. Many of those GI,s could attest to the dreadful scenes they witnessed.

My next tour of duty was on a converted air craft carrier in the South Pacific. The tide had turned dramatically for Japan. American soldiers and Marines' victories had largely swept Japanese forces from the western Pacific.

Although I have no outstanding heroics to boast about, I served my country honorably, and am proud to have done so. I began my tour of duty as an adventurous boy ready and eager to engage the enemy. After two years nine months and sixteen days of witnessing the sights, sounds, and smells of war, I came home a man.

So what is the point of one man's small contribution to an effort that almost everyone in America had participated in? From *Rosie the*

Riveter to the U.S.O. to the Waves and Wacs all the way up to the top brass? Everyone sacrificed in one way or another.

Patriotism and sacrifice had no equal to the Sullivan family from our heartland of Waterloo, Iowa. Not long after the bombing of Pearl Harbor, five Sullivan brothers enlisted in the U.S. Navy and wanted to be together on the same ship. The Navy granted their request. Their ship was sunk and the sea claimed all five brothers.

Without the sacrifice of so many mothers and fathers, wives, sisters, and brothers who lost their loved ones, we would not enjoy the peace and bounty we have now.

Now in the beginning of a new millennium the men of the last two generations, the high school and college graduates, have little knowledge of our history.

Ask a random group of young people any question posed about our nation's history, and in many cases it will result in a wrong answer or a blank stare.

Our national sense of patriotism and sacrifice has dramatically changed in my lifetime. Even the most significant national holidays are justified only by a day to take it easy, go to a ball game, or take a long weekend off of work.

PATRIOTISM! TODAY AND YESTERDAY

On August 14, 1945, Japan accepted the unconditional terms of surrender and World War II ended. We were victorious, and we prevailed because all of our citizens were bound by an emotion called patriotism.

Many prominent people joined the ranks of millions of Americans from all walks of life to fight for the cause of freedom. My generation just lost one of those patriots—**Ted Williams.** Anyone with a modicum of baseball lore knew him as the greatest hitter ever. What many do not know, (especially the younger generation), is that he enlisted in the Marine Corps and flew combat missions in the Pacific Theater of War. Had he not broken the continuity of his baseball career in WWII and the Korean War, he most likely would have shattered many of the records held by other of today's and yesterday's renowned hitters. The recent demise of one of Hollywood's most admired, James Stewart, also interrupted his career and he flew for the Army Air Corps. These are a but a few examples of true patriotism that I elaborated on more fully in my essay of, "Memoirs of WWII."

Now we find ourselves engaged in a war on terror. Engaged! Who? Who's engaged in what war? Us! All of us who went to that fireworks display at the park on the 4th of July. That's not our only contribution to the war effort. We're gonna show that stupid judge the proper way to recite the pledge of allegiance to our flag. You saw our illustrious leaders on the capital steps showing the way. Boy was that inspirational or what?

Grandstanding! Whataya mean grandstanding! Those guys are patriots! How about our recruiting stations? What about em? They kind of resemble that commercial on the tube about the Maytag repairman trying to cope with boredom.

The days of people leaving their jobs and careers to do battle with the bad guys are gone. In this day and age who wants to go out and face some fanatic who is willing to die for his cause. Yes! We do have some! Thank God for the young men and women who did show up at those recruiting stations.

As for the rest of us! Hey, we're fat and sassy! Who wants to give up the good life? And so it goes! Each generation claims a right to their standard of living. So who cares what happened fifty or a hundred years ago? This is the modern age. All that ancient history is repetitious and boring.

Anyway, Rukeyer's latest letter says the market is going to surge in the last half of 2002. Of course, that's all I needed to hear! **What the hell am I worried about?**

SEMPER FI! HEY JOE—SAY IT ISN'T SO!

"From the Halls of Montezuma, to the shores of Tripoli, we will fight our country's battles on the land and on the sea. First to fight for right and freedom and to keep our honor clean, we are proud to claim the title of the United States Marines."

It was bitter! It was hard to comprehend! Eighty Marines caught in a drug bust. Is nothing sacred anymore? Is honor really just not viable in our new modern age? Does the craving for money, no matter what the means, preclude any nobility of mind or action?

In another time and another place, I remember groups of Marines, survivors of Iwo Jima and Okinawa many with tears in their eyes singing, "The Marine Hymn" as they tried to forget the horrors they left behind, and were now receiving some well deserved R and R.

I had a cousin, "now deceased", "who eventually succumbed to the scars of battle on Tarawa. I wonder what his thoughts would be, as I know he was proud to serve in "The Corps".

There is no glory in war! But my memories of The Marines spearheading the invasion to recapture the Pacific Islands from well entrenched Japanese forces to secure our final victory is vivid in my memory bank. "The closest thing to glory" that I can think of, is the satisfaction of a victory achieved in a hard fought battle against an equally determined foe.

The U.S. Marines had a very distinguished history of service to our country since The Corps was founded by the Continental Congress in 1775. "The Corps" served our country with honor and distinction by providing troops trained for land, sea, and air operations.

Since The Corps was first established by an Act of Congress on July 11, 1798, the very essence that defines the qualities we want in those we choose to fight for and to preserve our freedoms are inherent in the "United States Marines".

To those of you who tarnished the honor of "The Corps" —SHAME!

Dogs: Precious Poodles, Mutts, and Special Breeds

For one brief shining moment I had a dog. It was a cute little pup of some unrecognizable heritage. This little pup caught my eye in a pet store and my Dad reluctantly succumbed to grant my wish to be master of this little beastie. The caveat was: *you take care of him.*

It didn't take long and he was no longer a pup. He did what dogs do, bark, growl, pee and poop, and he did it whenever and wherever he chose. He once chose to poop in our neighbor's flowerbed. Imagine! Our neighbor had the audacity to get mad! The satisfaction of owning and caring for Fido soon began to fade and I sold him to a kid who lived several blocks away for one buck. We lost $14 on that escapade.

The focus of my forthcoming criticism is not directed at dogs, but the dog owners who have lost or never had the responsible attitude to respect others' concerns when their dogs cause distress. I could write another book just on my life's encounters with canines and their masters. The point is whether people opt for mutts or dogs of distinction, many of them are attracted to fire plugs, lawns, flower beds, trees, parks, beaches, and all manner of areas where people go to frolic. The rude beasts even defecate in the same areas. Most of their masters frown upon such manners on **their** property.

The really perilous situations are the people that encounter the pit bulls, rottweilers, and diverse breeds, aggressive by nature and trained to attack, in the care of the careless and complacent master. Just about every week, we read or see these tragic events, when we watch the evening news and read our evening newspaper.

I am well aware that our canine pals contribute much needed services to our human needs and follies. Our olfactory senses are not in the same league as Fido's. We would be carted away to the nearest booby hatch, if we started sniffing luggage at Miami's or any airport for that matter. We would really look silly running to and fro keeping sheep from going astray, or seeking out a fireplug to pee on.

Our law officers know the value of Rex or Bruno when he or she takes a chunk out of some fiend's anatomy, and how about the Seeing Eye dog, a noble canine, worthy of our admiration! If *canis familiaris* can avoid coming under the spell of dog owners, who fit the classification of the sub-race known as *boobus Americanus* we will all be better off, and animosity between dog owners and non-dog owners will decrease.

MOVIES, PAST AND PRESENT

We went to neighborhood shows to see Buck Jones and Tom Mix. They were the good guys, along with their pals, mounted on fast palominos and mustangs chasing either Indians or rustlers. Their six shooters were blazing, miraculously getting off 20 to 30 rounds. It was exciting knowing that the bad Indians, (there were no good Indians in the movies in those days,) or the rustlers, were going to pay for their lawlessness. They were rounded up and shaken, but they never spilled any blood.

War movies were a little more graphic. The bad guys actually got killed, and some of the good guys too.

Flash Gordon supplied us with wonderment for 15 or 20 minutes as we waited for next week's episode to unfold and contemplate how he could survive the peril in his never ending battle against evil.

Then we had the comedies: Laurel and Hardy, (the fat guy and the skinny guy), The Three Stooges, and Our Gang. We left those Saturday matinees enthralled, usually staying for two shows.

The melodramas with the accompanying suspense, romance and conventionally happy ending usually resulted in leaving the theater with an uplifted feeling. You always felt gratified in the crime movies because the bad guys never won. How movies have changed!

Both the bad guys and the good guys now bleed a lot. Hollywood has decided we need a reality awakening. We must recognize that in the real world, crime quite often can be rewarding, especially concerning power and money. Now when we leave the cinema, we are reminded of what we already know, that our country and most of our planet, has a serious social problem.

Since men first crawled out of caves to pursue their careers, which were generally limited to hunting, fishing, gathering and avoiding being preyed upon by large beasts and other clans of club wielding brutes, mankind has always had its share of fiends and miscreants.

Alfred Hitchcock was a pacesetter, and Hollywood really got going with movies like *The Godfather* and *Saving Private Ryan* to show us in graphic detail what mankind is capable of.

Now we have the inevitable clash of opposing opinions as to how these graphic displays of eccentric behavior are affecting our psyche.

Not to be outdone the "Boobtube", is doing its best to traumatize our already neurotic disorders. On the tube, we can switch channels on our remote and choose sex, sex and violence, and a large variety of channels offering the viewer a chance to stare at inane presentations, along with an endless array of mind numbing commercials.

To be fair in my assessment of our collective foibles, I must admit there are some channels on TV that provoke serious thought. The news keeps us abreast of our irrational meanderings.

We can always rely on the Weather Channel to show us how violent the weather can be in our fair land. This is always a stimulus to disrupt the normal function of our dormant brain cells.

MOTORING, BEFORE AND AFTER THE INTERSTATE

Hey, let's go for a ride in the country…a spontaneous call for adventure on the open road! Remember those days, an **open road?** No traffic jams to impede our progress. No eighteen wheelers to intimidate us. It was a breeze to get out of the city.

It's the first day of June and before long we get the first scent of clover, sometimes mingled in with fresh cow manure. Ah, we're in the country experiencing just a simple little excursion for a couple of hours for a change of pace.

Sometimes on a weekend a picnic was the order of the day. That meant Uncle Charlie and Aunt Mami and brothers, sisters, and respective spouses assembled with their Chevys, Fords, and one Dusenberg, loaded down with food and a half-barrel of beer. Bats and softballs were included, as well as swimming suits because a lake was where we were headed.

If we were lucky no one got a flat tire on the way to our destination. We usually traveled in convoy in case someone needed assistance. My mom and dad had the oldest car, a Model A Ford. I learned to drive with my older brother as the teacher. We drove in the alleys to minimize any potential disaster during my learning period.

Holy Mackerel! How things have changed! Nobody goes for a drive in the country anymore. Just to get to the country from the city means fighting traffic jams to get out of the city. More gridlock going through the suburbs, next are exurbia's pitfalls, with road construction to accommodate one development after another.

So I find myself heading west out of Chicago with my nine-year-old grandson, "The What If Kid", at my side. "Grampa, what if we had a flat tire now? We would be up the creek with one of two lanes blocked off and no shoulder to pull off on," he exclaimed.

The *What-if Kid* is making me nervous with the possibility of a dinosaur or a saber toothed tiger coming out of that patch of woods. That could really cause chaos!

We are approaching what is referred to as the collar counties with their own growth difficulties to cope with. As we get closer to my destination to visit my old navy buddy, urban sprawl diminishes as we meld into rural sprawl. He likes the wide-open spaces, so he chose a five-acre estate to build on, along with about one hundred other families. It's called "Lost Lake Estates". They haven't built the lake yet, and it will be hard to find.

The "What If Kid" is studying the road map. He informs me that we are only about 65 miles from the Mississippi River.

After a pleasant visit with my buddy, I elect to get over to the interstate to get home faster. This is much better. We breeze along about 70 miles per hour while most people, anxious to get to wherever they are going, zip past us at 80 to 90 miles per hour.

"Hey Grampa, all those cars up ahead are stopped! There is road construction and one lane is closed! Nobody is moving! An eighteen wheeler tipped over causing a chain reaction with a seven car pileup," Ryan shouted.

"Grampa, look everybody's getting out of their cars! Some guys are fighting over there! One guy has a gun! Boy, some of them are acting like they are nuts!"

"That's road rage Ryan," I explained.

"Boy! A lot of people standing around sure look different than us. Look, that one guy over there has a towel wrapped around his head. Where do they all come from Grampa?"

"All over the world, Ryan," I answered.

"Why do they come over here?"

"It's too crowded where they came from," I told him.

SURVIVAL TACTICS IN NORTHERN WISCONSIN

The last week in November made its entry into Chicago with copious amounts of snow and temperatures near zero during the night. The year was 1932 and the depression had a firm grip on the nation. My Dad, Uncle Charlie, and brother-in-law Ed owned what passed for trucks in those days. They provided the necessities to "keep the wolf away from the door." These noble adventurers were loading up the trucks with balsam and spruce trees, which they had harvested out of the woods near Rhinelander, Wisconsin to be marketed in Chicago. As it turned out, they only broke even.

The tales that were told of their daring enterprise did not escape my ears. They did not dwell too much on the failure of that particular business enterprise, but their discourse on survival must have been comparable to a trek to the North Pole.

I had just celebrated my ninth birthday and I was enthralled by the stories of fleeting sightings of deer in the forest, as well as the wolves' howlings, which disturbed their sleep at night. They told of the relentless chant of the north wind as it penetrated the cabin, and stole the warmth of the fireplace consuming their cache of firewood. It was the last week of November and the snow threatened to stall their departure. But their derring-do prevailed and they headed home.

A few years after that event, twelve adults and five kids in our extended family made our way back to that very same cabin in the woods. Cots were set up side by side and the adults drew straws to see who would have the privilege of the use of the bed and bedroom during our long Labor Day weekend in the North Woods. The men fished, the women cooked, and the kids explored.

This was a New World, a new and different way of life. This was a wilderness, a land of enchantment. As our journey took us deeper into this forested land, I recall a restaurant where we stopped had a sign proclaiming: "If you don't eat, we both starve." Upon entering this establishment, another sign greeted us stating "This is the North Woods where men are men, and women are damned glad of it."

Boy! These people up here are tough and hardy! Someday I want to live up here!

The year was 1970 and my energies were directed into the completion of a cabin on Little Sand Lake where my wife, Lorraine and I could escape on long weekends. It was good to get away from the ever-increasing maddening crowds of a metropolitan area.

Eventually, we sold the cabin and purchased a home on a little pine-fringed lake, seven miles north of Eagle River, Wisconsin. This was to be our retirement home. At age sixty, I elected to quit the rat race, take early retirement, and join those intrepid pioneers in the hinterlands. We soon realized that the use of a fireplace insert was a necessity in order to offset high heating costs. We gained occupancy the first week of October. Snow squalls were becoming more frequent. I began to supplement our firewood supply with frequent trips to logging areas as winter was fast approaching.

The weeks went by, the temperature fell, and snow and our first Christmas arrived. We harvested our own Christmas tree from a nearby woods. Christmas vacation prompted my daughter to load up her car with the kids and gifts to join us for our first winter's activities that included tobogganing, ice fishing, and feeding the fireplace as winter set in with a vengeance.

My daughter and kids headed home and Lor and I relaxed and fed the fire. I awoke on January 15th and checked the outside temperature—34° below zero. I went out to the garage to see if the four-wheel drive truck would start. It did as I had an electric heater going full blast directed at the engine block.

By the time I got back to the house, my face felt like stone covered with frost. My feet were already cold after just a few minutes exposure. Then it dawned on me. The wind was howling like a banshee. Factoring in the wind chill, it was probably close to *absolute zero* outside. This pioneering life was proving to be challenging. My son called from Downers Grove, Illinois, concerned about our survival as it was 23° below in his domain. Within a few days, the temperature began to moderate and it finally settled at 5° below zero at night and 10° above during the day, but it also brought more snow.

If you did not drive a pickup truck with a gun rack in the back, you were not a genuine woodsman. You were probably a flatlander. We did not hibernate in the winter. We thoroughly enjoyed ice fishing, skiing, skating, and the camaraderie of visits with friends and neighbors of the same persuasion.

Summers had a special allure. The pine-scented air, cool to mild days and cool evenings were a delight. No air conditioning was required. Our little sixty-three acre lake provided us with pan fish, bass, and northern pike. Beavers and otters made the lake their home as well. As the months and years went by, subtle changes were taking place.

Northern Wisconsin was becoming a magnet for people fleeing the crime and congestion in the cities to our south. Homes and cottages were being built on 5 acre, 20 acre, and 40-acre parcels, as well as lakefront property. Exxon discovered copper on a large tract of land and soon exploited this forest to start an open pit copper mine.

The Northwoods was losing its identity! Built in restrictions to retain the ecological qualities of the land and water were being compromised. Pristine areas were being corrupted to what we generally consider progress. We chose Florida as our next retirement realm. It was disheartening to see the allure of the Northwoods diminish.

WHATEVER HAPPENED TO ROMANCE?

The nightingale tells his fairy tale, and I am once again with you, when our love was new and each kiss an inspiration.

But that was long ago. Yes, it was long ago. Those love ballads of yesteryear such as "Stardust", Hoagy Carmichael's classic, and the memorable"The Nearness of You", don't exist anymore, not in this modern age.

Those two songs were but a small representation of so many great examples of popular music that folks of my generation enjoyed. Those tunes inspired a culture of courtship and romantic rituals.

The culture of courtesy and chivalry directed especially toward the fair sex probably reached its apex when Sir Walter Raleigh displayed his gallantry by placing his cloak over a puddle to allow Queen Elizabeth graceful access to her carriage. Gallantry of this caliber has long been lost in the fog of antiquity. However, when we have music replete with lyricism and charm, combined with a culture embracing gracious manners as the norm, we have a perfect stimulus for romance.

Holding hands in the movies, entranced by Nelson Eddy and Jeanette McDonald's melodramatic portrayal of their romantic involvement, would be considered real cornball stuff in today's post-modern boorish attitudes.

Dancing cheek to cheek has been replaced by a new standard that perpetuates a current lifestyle consistent with the debasement of the female gender—dirty dancing.

The demise of romance bespeaks of today's acceptance of coarseness and the reticence to

accept propriety is all too evident when you consider the adulation of the rap artist, *Eminem*. His collection of awards, golden statues and the sale of millions of his CDs, consisting of repellent and trashy words, which can hardly be considered lyrics are a testimony to the vulgarity, commonly accepted as art.

This boorish behavior cannot be solely attributed to *Eminem* and his ilk. In today's culture, the ladies are not without their immersion in our current culture of a transition to a lower level of moral behavior.

Traditionally, the ritual of going on a date would be the accompaniment of a young woman at the bequest of a young man desirous of her company. The date could be dinner and dancing, going to a movie, or a theater, or a visit to an ice cream parlor. Usually, this gallant gesture was the young man's financial responsibility.

The merits of dating seem to be replaced by "hanging out", (a meeting place), be it a bar, comedy club, or whatever. Boy meets girl and they "hook up". These liaisons are usually without commitment of any kind and are emotionally barren.

Moonlight and love songs seem to be out of date.

I'll take romance.

4

The Blithe Spirit

PEOPLE HAVE THEIR FUN IN MANY STRANGE WAYS

In the privacy of our homes, and when we leave the sanctuary of our abodes, most people enjoy good fun. Let's consider some of the dumb, malicious, idiotic and dreadful things people do for fun.

Starting with dumb fun…how about motorboats and jet skis racing around various waterways with no apparent objective? These are usually the people who create a hazard to themselves and other more responsible boats and swimmers. Many manatees have sustained injuries and died as a result of these yahoos. Dirt bikes and off road vehicles make a big contribution to environmental degradations. And what about the fun of losing our money in casinos and playing the lottery. Who was it who said "a sucker is born every minute?"

Malicious fun…the shooting of animals, legal and illegal, the arsonists who start fires in buildings and forests. People, young and old, who revel in taunting people who don't fit in.

Idiotic fun…Russian roulette, and the fun people have by all the acts of vandalism the human mind can summon up. The various rock band type concerts and Woodstock type happenings that appear to be a mix of idiocy, malicious and dumb fun.

Dreadful fun…I must preface the following by the uncertainty of what the perpetrators of the acts actually feel if not fun. Derailing trains, dropping huge rocks on passing vehicles, and shooting people indiscriminately.

I could go on and on, but the bottom line as I see it is, we have hordes of people out there whose intellect is about 10 points above fungi.

THE BASEBALL SAGE, JOE SIX PACK

They have been with us when we first heard the ump shout that all inspiring phrase, "Play Ball!" It's the seventh inning, but Joe Six Pack does not get up for the seventh inning stretch. He can't. His energy level is almost depleted. He is our modern day all knowing master of baseball wisdom. His team is performing like a minor league outfit of one-arm ball players. He did not go to the ballpark today. He's watching the game on the tube.

He cannot understand why the manager started with that rookie southpaw when the Podunk Polecats have 6 out of 9 right-handed batters. Now here it is the seventh inning and that stupid manager's got a reliever warming up with a 4.04 earned run average. Well we've still got a chance, we're only 4 runs behind and it's the top of the seventh.

"Honey, will you get me another Bud out of the fridge? Well they blew that inning! The first guy draws a walk, second guy pops up, and dum dum Danny hits into a double play. That jerk shoulda been sent to the minors along time ago. I knew it! They got two more runs off that rookie. That dumb, stupid pitching coach is dumber than the manager. Geez! The last of the eighth and our jerks are 6 runs behind. Well, we got three runs in the last of the eighth, thanks to the error of that yo yo second baseman of the Polecats. Well, it's the ninth inning and we're three runs behind. Honey, another Bud please?"

"Joe, you gotta watch your weight!"

"I am! I lost two pounds, I'm down to 298 now."

"But Joe, you're only five foot five!"

"Aw c'mon honey, one more Bud. We held em, first inning since the 5th that they didn't score. That reliever did the trick, he's the guy I would a used. Holy mackerel two outs, bases loaded and who do they bring in to pinch-hit for the pitcher? They use that jerk with only a 232 batting average against right-handed pitchers. Honey, Jimmy Jeepers just hit a grand slam homer. He's the guy I woulda put in!"

That's our boy folks! The six pack guzzling *boobus Americanus* male who doesn't know an Allen wrench from a Phillips-head screwdriver, or an outhouse from a bidet. This fellow watches professional sports and feeds the egos and wallets of overpaid athletes. His reason for watching is not as much for entertainment as it is for his need to fantasize about being the athlete he could never become.

THE GOOD, THE BAD, AND THE UGLY IN BASEBALL

I always had the impression that the baseball players I knew as a boy growing up in Chicago in the 30's and 40's played for the love of the game and a good measure of loyalty to their fans. This translated to most ball players remaining on the same team for most of their careers.

In the 50's and 60's, the post-war years, not-so-subtle changes began to take place. The **big** syndrome in our culture began to manifest itself in baseball and sports in general. A talented sports figure now is more prone to play for the highest bidder. The highest bidder is the owner with deep pockets.

Some baseball stadiums enjoy packed houses and some are half-empty. Most of the talented players are not playing out of loyalty to a specific group of adoring fans, or the city or town they most admire. Hell no! They're businessmen! They like the color of green and big bucks!

So what is the impetus that inspires the average fan to deplete his financial resources to enlarge his hero's coffers, already abounding in greenbacks? When you consider the cost of a ducat to enter the hallowed grounds our idols frolic in, and what you pay for a beer and a hot dog, it causes me to wonder where is the logic?

Sixty years ago memory lane was replete with the ballplayers, who were held in high regard because they fit the mold of a Cal Ripken.

Today we read about these grossly overpaid prima donnas getting into trouble with the law for various misdemeanors and felonies, and then glossed over by their managers as, "Boys will be boys."

My guess as to why the stadiums are a magnet for fans of our national past time is primarily what it has always been…the draw of an exceptional talent. The house that Ruth built pretty much defines the appeal. Guys like Bob Feller, Jackie Robinsion, Hank Aaron, Roger Clemens Sandy Koufax, Willy Mays, Mickey Mantle, Lou Gehrig, Mark McQuire, Sammy Sosa, and many others. There will always be the bad guys to tarnish the image and sour the sweetness of the sound of the crack of the bat.

In the July issue, 2001 of *Sporting News*, there are 23 professional baseball players listed, starting with Cal Ripken, who have devoted their time to community service. Ripken and others on this list have made generous monetary contributions and enhanced the perception that baseball does have an ample supply of good guys by a variety of their noble deeds.

As long as we have gifted athletes who possess honor and venerate the fans who are in awe of their prowess, our national past time and other sports will not lose their appeal.

Lest we forget, Joe Six Pack goes to the ballpark from time to time. He and his ilk are scattered throughout the ballpark swilling beer, shouting expletives, and in general being disruptive and becoming a nuisance. You know this jerk; he is the guy two rows behind you. He knows and uses all the four letter obscenities we were not taught in grammar school English class. But your little guy in the seat next to you is all ears as he gets a lesson in profanity.

YA GOTTA BE A FOOTBALL HERO

"Coach Skullnik, here's the new kid I been tellin' ya about."

"Hello, kid. Welcome to the Pro's!"

"How ya doin', Coach, how ya doin?"

"I'm fine, kid." Frank, this is our new *All American* from Neolithic U.

"In the flesh. Just what you need to beef up that puny offensive line."

"C'mon! Our offensive line averages 380 pounds."

"Well, this kid's still growing and he tips the scales at 522 pounds—*in the buff.*"

"Are you ready to *rock 'em and sock 'em*, kid?"

"You betcha! You betcha!"

"What did you major in at school, kid?

"Duhhh, language arts, Coach."

"And what language are you most fluent in?"

"*Trash talk*, Coach!"

"Frank, according to this list of five guys we drafted out of college, his name is Clive Arlington Brougham. His name just doesn't seem to fit."

"He was an orphan, Coach." The Brougham family from Connecticut's upper crust found him as a child wandering naked in the *River of No Return* wilderness area in Idaho where they have a lodge."

"Get that other kid, the other All American we got from Neolithic U last year. You know, Semanthohua Kennumphaah. Bring him over here so he can introduce Clive to the team and get suited up. We got anything big enough for this guy?"

"Yeah, Coach, but it all had to be special made."

"You think he'll make a good offensive lineman?"

"Absolutely! No matter how many showers he takes, he still has a distinctively gamey odor. The guys on the defensive line have to contend with *that* and his bulk. He'll be All Pro the first year. He's a natural for offense."

"How tall is the kid? He never stands straight up. He's always hunched over. His knuckles touch the ground and he's not even in a crouch."

"I really don't know, but he is tall. I saw him stand straight once in a college game I was scouting. A strong safety tried to rush the quarterback. He grabbed the safety, picked him up and threw him into the stands! He got penalized for unnecessary roughness."

Three games into the pre-season, Coach Skullnik is all smiles. The squad is jubilant. They won all three games and the sports writers heaped on the praise. The quarterbacks never got sacked. The rookie, Clive, was any coach's dream. His tendency to snarl and drool when his adrenalin was up, created panic in the opposing team.

The coach asked his first string quarterback, Spangler Chauncy Sesphul, a Harvard graduate and Rhodes Scholar, "What do you think of Clive?"

"He dah man!"

Coach Skullnik, always open to second opinions, asked his high school phenom back-up quarterback, Roosevelt Franklin, "How do you assess Clive?"

"He doesn't respond to audibles, but it doesn't matter. He does everything by instinct. He has an innate sense of primordial reactionary contumacy thereby exacerbating his fervor for the impending encounter in the trenches. He was born for this sport. He has no equal!"

"What are they calllin' Clive?"

"Big Foot!"

FANCIFUL FLIGHTS OF FANTASY

We collectively fall under the spell, when the glamour of Hollywood's beautiful people bewitch us into viewing the annual award ceremony of "Who gets the Oscar?"

Who but the populous of our great nation would stay up late glued to the tube to succumb to our propensity toward the hypnotic spell of whimsy. The Brits may even surpass us when it comes to capricious capers.

Now I will not deny that movies can be very entertaining and I succumb to this art form and go, "to the show" from time to time when I read a critique by those who make "big bucks" analyzing this stuff to enhance our knowledge of the human persona.

As is our bent, movies are bigger, louder, more violent, more sexy, more profane, more thought provoking, more stupid in short, more of everything. What really bugs me is when these movie critics convince me to see a movie that their analytical genius touts as a three or four star creative achievement. To wit:

My wife and I just recently spent four and a half senior citizen dollars apiece at our local cinema to sit through three hours of boring banality called (About a Boy). How did Hugh Grant ever make it to the big screen?

Let's focus on the tube, the medium that consumes so much of our time, to provide the wherewithal to deplete our brains of the nutrients we need to promote healthy mentality. In other words, watching too much TV can make you brain dead, especially when you are subjected to the repetitive banal crap we refer to as commercials. We recently moved to an area in central Florida where we subscribed to satellite, "Direct TV". (Cable TV is not available in our area),

We now have at our fingertips, (the remote), that device where we can scan more channels than we ever dreamed of to addle our brains. All of this happy horsepucky and then we have the added bonus of not having to dislodge the contentment of our languid repose.

How many times have you tuned in your car radio to find some music to "soothe the savage beast," and then give up in frustration when all you get is modern age noise? Do not despair; our new modern age technology is going to bestow upon us 100 channels of more noise and blather. It's coming folks. It's XM satellite radio! Wow it's bigger and it's awesome!

Oh! Let's not be so negative! We are not devoid of worthwhile entertainment. The tube will not let us down. Football will replace baseball, and the testosterone levels of the couch potatoes watching their heroes trying to decapitate the other team's quarterback will reach new heights as we fall under the spell of football madness.

Ah! But when it comes to fury and rage to titillate our obsession with antics of the savage beast, what could be more entertaining than the lusty world of (so-called) professional wrestling.

Ah, sweet mystery of life at last I found thee!

5

Land of Enchantment

FLORIDA—LAND OF SUNSHINE, BUGS, THUNDERSTORMS AND OLD TIMERS

My wife and I became permanent residents of Florida in September of 1989. From November to mid May, Florida's climate is idyllic. From mid May through October, Florida's good nature gets sidetracked. As the summer solstice approaches our latitudes, heat and humidity, bugs, ants, spiders, and various types of mold and fungi make their presence known. Almost everyday thunderstorms, flash floods and hurricanes threaten and her natural charm begins to fade. The permanent occupants of our joyous land seek sanctuary in our air-conditioned abodes.

Those that venture out soon become afflicted by the heat and humidity and begin to display erratic behavior. Friday and Saturday nights are the usual times people congregate at their favorite restaurants and watering holes, when two for one drinks are offered, and people and their cars take on a new form of adventure in the summer. Similar adventures and other forms of frivolity and adverse behavior become more prevalent. Teenage vandalism, always in vogue in Florida, becomes more original and prolific as our future leaders leave the confines of our centers of learning. When they venture out and Florida's merciless sun rearranges their brain cells, their misadventures take on destruction comparable to the last days of Pompeii.

Florida's contribution to the new millennium was ushered in by the *Elian* fiasco that resulted in Florida's ignoble perception. The idiocy of that event, depriving the boy of being returned to his father is an example of Florida's lunatic fringe. Florida's balloting and political madness in last November's presidential election precludes any more enlightenment on Florida's political misadventures. On the federal level of deficient reasoning, the *powers that be* in Washington added to Florida's troublesome political gaffes. The U.S. Coast Guard has been assigned the task of intercepting Cuban boat people before they reach Florida's shores. If the Coast Guard fails in this endeavor, the Cubans, in essence, become privy to American citizenship by their elusive tactics.

My gut feeling is that our salubrious climate is the catalyst for the apparent lunacy that prevails the closer you get to the Banana Republic of Miami. I have contemplated moving elsewhere, but I am afraid Florida's contagion is spreading nationwide. Hope always springs eternal, despite a cranky old grouch's emphasis on the negative.

FLORIDA'S DUMB STUFF—IT'S OUTRAGEOUS!

The ludicrous happenings never seem to end in this land of toil and sin. We are on the fast track to catch up to that great booby hatch on the West Coast.

Our most recent award for deficient mental activity took place during July, 2001. It was on TV, in our local newspaper, and had gained national attention. The dilemma involves our dear flag, *Old Glory*. The controversy centered around a marine veteran who raised his American flag on a twelve-foot pole. This event took place in the town of Jupiter, which is highly self-regarded as a community of *the elite*.

Some people in the community have no quarrel with this man's display of patriotic zeal. Many apparently take umbrage with this man's devotion, since it is in violation of the Homeowners Association covenants. As of this writing, he is fighting this in court and being fined 100 dollars per day for each day he flies the flag on the flagpole.

Hundreds of people are rallying to his side in what they believe is a travesty by the judge in this *cause celebre*. War veterans are coming from far and wide to attend rallies and marches. The court hearing is forthcoming and promises to be well attended.

The disparity of laws on the books concerning our flag is really striking a nerve here. We have discontents desecrating our flag in so many ways, yet this is condoned as a right of free expression.

The last expression in defiance of Florida law and disrespect to our flag, (to my knowledge), was during the discontent when Elian Gonzales was reunited with his father. Many of the Cuban and Cuban American malcontents in the their enclave of Miami demonstrated their contempt for our laws by burning the flag. This was glossed over by Florida's pandering elected officials, ever mindful to avoid offending an active voting community.

Remember folks, just because they did not get their way and got a little rebellious going ballistic in the streets, it's just an expression of free speech. It's nothing to get upset about, especially if you need their vote at election time.

Although the relatives of Elian Gonzales retained the boy in defiance of US and international law, one US Senator from Florida even characterized Elian's relatives as a *typical American family*. **How's that for pandering?**

Spin Doctors and Developers Exacerbating Florida's Environmental Concerns

There is a constant supply of developers exploiting our natural resources to their advantage. They are becoming more adept in the use of perfidious guile to give the impression of being environmentally compatible.

The use of misleading ploys is beneficial to them, in that a gullible public will be taken in by their wiles. Twisting things around is always a concern no matter what the subject. With environmental concerns becoming more pervasive with the population explosion in our realm, they are masters of the spin zone.

With snowbirds finding sanctuary from the blizzards up north, and illegal immigrants finding their way to our shores, buildable land and wetlands are under siege. Most of the developments need retention ponds to help alleviate flooding. They refer to these as lakes and, in many instances, they drain the wetlands. Traditionally, Florida is, especially in the south, known for its wetlands. Florida's unique plant life and wildlife are being pushed out of their natural habitat with no place to go. Is this what we consider progress?

The last few years we have experienced some destructive brush and forest fires due to severe drought conditions. Many people are of the opinion that droughts in Florida will become more prevalent. The reasoning is the dwindling wetlands. The natural evaporative cycle of ground water is disrupting normal weather patterns by a reduction in rainfall.

I have only been a resident here since 1989. The native residents and those that have called Florida home for decades can attest to the loss of wetlands, pollution of lakes, rivers and yes, even coastal waters.

To our dismay we have many public officials in the developers sphere of influence, exacerbating Florida's morass.

THE CALAMITY OF NEGLIGENCE

I don't know what kind of people work for Florida's *Department of Children and Families*. They certainly seem to be beset by inefficient employees. To say they are lax in attending to duty is an understatement, but to say criminal intent is involved is too strong. Somewhere in between lies a real and disturbing problem.

I have made a point of stating that most of us are not privy to the knowledge that people in power possess. We read and hear the news, but what goes on behind the curtain, we will never know.

The case of 5-year-old Riyla Wilson is consistent with the deplorable state of the indolent disposition of the DFC's personnel. Little Rilya Wilson disappeared from state care 15 months before she was reported missing. As of this date, June 24, 2002, according to an article in *The Ledger*, a newspaper serving Polk County, Florida, 1237 children under state care cannot be located. How's that for a casual attitude regarding child welfare?

If that's not enough to raise your hackles, maybe this will! The following are excerpts from *The Ledger*, dated June 23, 2002:

Five years ago, the ROE children, five brothers and their sister emerged battered but alive from the grasp of state approved Foster parents who locked them in a room, beat them regularly and fed them a diet of *Nyquil* and cereal soaked on *Kool-Aid*. The following excerpt describes what these 6 children endured at the hands of of Jackie and John Lynch, the Foster parents. The children's ages are: Jesse, 15; twins Jordan and Joseph, 14; Toby, 12: and Twins Suzanna and Robbie, 9.

Except for beatings, meager feedings, and erratic days at school, the children rarely left the small room that made up their world from 1990 to 1997.

Occasionally, Jordan or Joseph would slip out of the locked room through a window near the top of the door and rummage for food to bring back to the others. They were caught and beaten, and the Lynches covered the opening with wire.

After attorney Howard Talenfeld filed a suit on behalf of the Roe children against DCF in 1999, documents surfaced that indicate the agency had evidence that the Lynch home was not a safe place for children.

Records showed that Jackie Lynch's daughter from a prior marriage was removed from her care in 1987 for sexual and emotional abuse. Frank Lynch had an arrest record for obstruction of justice and owed $16,000 in child support payments to his own biological children. And *as a teenager living with the young Roes, Michael Lynch was arrested after he videotaped himself having sex with a 14 year old girl.*

The children said Michael beat them and often shoved Joseph or Jordan inside a plastic crate, taped it shut and threw it in the pool as the boy struggled for air.

"I used to think—I'm going to die," said Jordan.

Talenfeld argued that the children's constitutional right to safety had been violated by the DCF.

"It's impossible for me to comprehend that anyone could torture these six beautiful children," said Talenfeld.

The Lynches paid a $140 fine and now live in Alabama.

All six if the Roe siblings agree they survived the ordeal by looking out for one another.

"We stuck together," said Jordan. "We depended on Jesse. He kept track of us, kept us in line."

"I didn't know I had that responsibility," said Jesse, 15. "I didn't know what a normal life was."

The basketball player is learning to drive and wants to be a Navy Seal.

Since becoming part of the Rodrigues family, the children go to school and spend time camping, boating, and eating chili cheese dogs. Memories of the Lynch years linger, but they are safely shared among family. I've tried to put everything behind me," says Jesse. "There's a lot more to do than be stuck in a room."

They are now in the care of Kathy and Rod Rodrigues who left a 21 year career to become a full time Foster parent.

To fathom the depths of Florida's idiosyncrasies is challenging, to say the least. Here's another article by Brian Bandell of the Associated Press for you, dear reader to ponder the vapid state of affairs here in *Wonderland.*

Bush: No Grand Jury for Missing Children

MIAMI—Gov. Jeb Bush has refused to create a statewide grand jury to investigate the 1,237 children under state care who can't be located.

The Department of Children & Families has classified most of these children as either runaways, out-of-state or taken from their homes by either by a family or relative. None of them were visited in May.

State Rep. Frederica Wilson, D-Miami said the department need to account for these children to make sure thy haven't gone missing like 5-year old Rilya Wilson, who disappeared from state care 15 months before she was reported missing.

She said the proposal is supported by the Florida Black Caucus and the other members of the state government.

Wilson sent several letters to Bush and called his office asking to meet with him and discuss a grand jury. She said she didn't receive a response.

At a fund-raiser Saturday, Bush said he was aware of her requests, but denied them choosing to stick with the recommendations of a Blue Ribbon Panel that he appointed to investigate the DCF.

"We've taken the recommendations of the Blue Ribbon Panel and we're moving on to improve the system," Bush said.

Wilson said the panel's recommendations were already included in the DCF's guidelines for years, but they've never been followed. A grand jury would be more effective, she said, because it could subpoena people to testify.

Bush downplayed the number of children the DCF hasn't visited and said that no investigation is needed.

I Need a Vacation—You Pick Up the Tab!

It's known as cultural exchange, or international relations. Whatever spin our elite legislators contrive, it is to have us believe that the junkets they have a propensity for, is for our benefit. Yes, some may have some merit. But how many are wasteful? Does extravagance and self-indulgence take place on our tax money, or are they thrifty, keeping in mind that "waste not, want not" is also for our benefit?

Remember we want to balance the budget, don't we? But good relations are vital to our interests. Those foreign big shots have *savoir-faire*.

Our guys and gals can't go traipsing around on their hallowed ground on nickels and dimes and appearing deficient in worldly affairs. Statesmanship requires big bucks!

However, the fleecing of America is all too evident when we are made aware of our legislator's penchant for the ostentatious inclination that impels a desire for foreign travel.

Our news media is keeping us posted on Florida's Secretary of State, Katherine Harris.

The following is a part of an editorial in the *Stuart News,* published on August 6, 2001, regarding her lavish spending habits.

> *On her watch, the Secretary of State's Office international-relations budget rose from $783,000 in fiscal 1999 to $3.4 million in fiscal 2001. (As part of the review committee deal, the House and Senate funded the program at the same level this year). During her first 22 months in office, Harris amassed $106,000 in personal travel bills on visits to Argentina, Australia, Barbados, Brazil, Canada, Mexico, Panama and Venezuela.*
>
> *Perhaps the review committee will validate Harris' assertion that the good feelings her trips engender to foreign government leaders and cultural dignitaries are vital to a strong Florida economy. If that's the case, the hope must be that the committee members explain how average Floridians, who cannot afford such junkets, might have trouble seeing the connection.*
>
> *If the committee, on the other hand, validates the suspicion that Harris' understanding of economic development is imperfect, legislative leaders should cancel her international-relations program next year.*
>
> *As for Harris herself, she'll most likely be fine. In 2003, her elective office is scheduled to sunset under the state's reorganization plan. She's expected to run for Congress, where junketeering is a high art. If she wins, her opportunities for lavish foreign travel on someone else's nickel should increase geometrically.*

DISGRUNTLED EMPLOYEES, TOTIN GUNS

"The tattoo on his arm said it all." That was the first sentence of an article in our local paper about another tragic episode of the never-ending gun violence, which we have all become accustomed to. "Proud Daddy", that was the second sentence, referring to the tattoo.

The story continues regarding William White, 33 years old, and father of 3 shot to death on the job site by a coworker, who took exception to the task he was assigned to. Another worker remains in critical condition by the shooter carrying an AK 47 rifle. The third potential victim survived. The gun jammed.

The distraught family members are now left to cope with a tragedy we read about, and witness on TV with frequent regularity of the boss getting shot by a gun toting nut ready to snuff out a life without a second thought.

I have an acquaintance that is employed by a large catalog company in a managerial position. He has expressed his concern to his superiors of the "Braggadocio", of some of the people in his department regarding their cache of firearms. This is usually enlarged upon when they take issue with the work orders assigned to them. The response by his superiors is, "You're making a mountain out of a mole hill."

William White's widow, still in a state of disbelief, lamented, "I can't believe anything like this could happen!" This is the haunting refrain from every widow or mother who has endured a similar misfortune.

The bottom line here is most working families are too busy working and trying to keep their head above water in trying economic times to dwell on the ever present gun violence in our nation.

The news media, (except in the local area), doesn't give random shootings much coverage anymore because it is so common place. On a national level, you might find a small report on the fourth or fifth page. The exception would be if the shooting were in the form of a massacre.

HANG IN THERE, YOU OLD BUZZARDS

A time for calm and a time for panic! Lethargy usually sets in shortly after lunch and that drowsy feeling succumbs to a little siesta. For a while that tranquil feeling takes over and the sandman does his thing. Suddenly, you're awakened! The rescue squad again; the sirens whine full blast. Another old-timer bites the dust. The serenity is gone. Panic disorients you. You wonder if it's the guy with the cane you see from time to time. He's one year younger than you are.

That's life here in the slow lane, the geriatric domain. Those rescue squad guys don't get much time to relax.

The gold in "the golden years" has been fleeced. Oh yes, no time clock to punch, time to pursue flights of fancy, hobbies, and travel. We do have at least that silver lining. But as the years go by and we are nowhere to be seen in the obituary columns, we still have concerns.

Most of our investments have fallen short of our hopes and expectations. So how will this affect our standard of living? Numerous ads find their way to our mailbox touting the benefits of health food supplements for "geezers". The people depicted are gray haired without the usual lines and blemishes, and have miraculously retained a youthful body attired in fashionable rompers, ready for a few rounds of tennis. Ponce De Leon, it's not a fountain, but it's for real. Oh yeah!

Now we can allay our fears of losing our health and appearance, as long as we stick to that new diet and all that health food stuff, and don't forget to exercise instead of taking another nap.

Sometimes the mailman delivers a real whammy. We read the first few lines. "Can you, will you be able to afford nursing home care?" We stare in disbelief as the next sentence contains words like walker, wheelchair, beds designed for old people, that's us!

Last but not least, how will our final days play out? Nobody knows!

The scam artists here in Florida, (and we have them in abundance), are hard at work to relieve our fears. It is a challenge for seniors to avoid their clutches. They have charisma and charm. They are devious and cunning, kind of like lawyers and politicians.

The warnings on TV and our local newspapers keep us abreast of these fallen angels, some who have made the mistake of trying to bilk some savvy senior out of his life's savings, aware of their seductive methods. But alas! There is always another to fill the void while these devious devils of deceit are now known to the public, as they try to stay out of the pokey. And so the saga continues in our land of enchantment.

6

Bewitched, Bothered and Bewildered

Only in America

You will find in the Deep South and deep in the heart of Texas, dry counties, land of the *self-righteous bible thumpers*, who would deny you a cold beer to quench your thirst after enduring a 108 degree day. But if you want to purchase another, *shootin' iron or ammo*, for your semi-automatic rifle and a kit to convert it into an automatic rifle (because your eyesight is bad and it will make it easier to shoot that buck), *There's no problem.* The preacher knows the location of all the gun shops.

When football season starts in Dixieland, they have a hotline to heaven as they huddle over the pigskin and implore for divine help to *win that game.* It's great to have such an all-consuming passion that can transcend the important issues that people pray about such as deliverance from natural disasters and all the forms of dementia that abounds in our realm.

Can anyone explain why we have posted speed limits on our interstates? When I find myself setting the cruise control for the posted speed limit, I must get into the far right lane or be blown off the road. The *big rigs, eighteen wheelers*—**Wow!**—they'll pick you up and spit you out if you don't hang on as they pass you like you're standing still.

Stay outta that courtroom; you don't wanna see **dah judge!** You know—that guy that makes his entry into that hallowed hall of justice with his robes swirling in all their magnificence. You never know what he has up his sleeve.

If you do have the misfortune to appear before this person of such distinguished rank, be sure to get a good mouthpiece, someone who can articulate with the best. If you have to rely on a public defender or some yokel who cannot enunciate, "You're doomed." Try to appear before Judge Casper Milquetoast for a slap on the wrist for your dastardly behavior. If the fickle finger of fate sticks you with a clone of Judge Roy Bean no matter who defends you, you'll be lucky if you're not in solitary for a week on, "piss and punk." On the other hand, if he is in a benevolent mood, you might only get five years in the slammer with nothing to live on but food and water, all because you forgot to signal for that left turn and that rear burned out tail-light.

Human brain malfunctioning is evident in just about every region of our planet by hordes of people with afflicted brain cells causing discontent. Makes you wonder if the whole world isn't just one, *big booby hatch*. But this is *where we live*, and must contend with an over abundance of our citizens afflicted with bizarre behavior. It's kind of scary to think about the world leaders, at least those considered our friends, expecting us to lead in maintaining sanity in our so called civilization when so many in our domain are in that class called, *Boobus Americanus*. If a segment of society known to have some people with some screws loose is normal, when does it become abnormal?

The TV bible thumpers hammer away constantly on our peculiar emotional disturbances. Most of them seem to think Satan should take the rap for this deviant conduct. They might be right! He is already a charter member in the N.R.A. cult and has aspirations to be the next Speaker of the House.

PERFIDY

It's July 11, 2002, ten months to the date since the horror of the terrorist attacks on our country. The hue and cry of our *Commander in Chief* resounded across the land. "Osama Bin Laden, you evil son of a gun; **We're gonna getchya!**"

Well we haven't caught him yet. The dummies think he's hiding in a cave. Baloney! They haven't considered the obvious. Here are three possibilities the FBI should seriously look into:

- He's working as a baggage handler at Chicago O'Hare airport.

- He has a Mom and Pop motel in Philadelphia.

- He's working for our immigration department.

But with the all the hand wringing and anxiety about these evil forces of Osama and his cohorts, we have to contend with our own breed of evil doer's equally determined to wreck havoc on our country, by the twin character flaw so dominant by many of our citizens. Hypocrisy and greed are alive and flourishing, especially among the elite and powerful.

Day by day, week by week, the DOW, S&P, and the NASDAQ hit new lows as last year's miracle companies and their stalwart CEO's are exposed as fraudulent and mercenary schemers.

One market strategist proclaims, "This market has completely broken the spirit of investors," What a revelation! With the trust in investment managers, stockbrokers, blue chip companies and their CEO's shattered, who in the hell wouldn't have their spirits broken? Another analyst tells us that we are downtrodden. Gee whiz! Why should we be downtrodden? Just because we have sustained losses of 40 to 60 percent of our investments that our managers declared as the way to go for our retirement years? Then read or listen to the banality of the crap these marvels of the financial world foist upon us. The futility in this regard is so apparent since none of them know what will happen in 5 minutes, let alone tomorrow, next week, month, or year.

One thing we can count on is that *the status quo* is not likely to change much if at all. The robber barons of today will build their ostentatious multimillion-dollar estates.

It will be interesting to see what kind of punishment is meted out to these tarnished toads. I wonder how many of the smart crooks among the elite will never get caught as they continue to plunder, as our trust in the system wanes.

Since our Commander in Chief and his Prince Regent are now under scrutiny for supposed hanky panky regarding their past dealings in the shady world of finance, who are we to question the validity of equal justice for all.

After all we are just *the folks*, not the elite in our land that seems to be ever drifting from a democracy to a plutocratic society.

LAWS FOR THEM AND LAWS FOR US

Most civilized societies have many laws that their citizens are expected to abide by. If you go afoul of the law, you are punished or penalized for your wrong behavior. That is, if you get caught for your unlawful conduct. If you reside in an uncivilized community where the laws are less complex—and you go astray, punishment is simply *Death by Booka*. Justice is swift!

Ah! But here in the good old USA, the laws are administered, or not administered by what classification you are in.

> **Category #1:** The ordinary folks, the working stiffs, the guy or gal and the retirees who got suckered into the stock market by listening to their financial wizard. Don't miss the stop sign or get caught going 50 m.p.h. in a 40 m.p.h. zone or you will get hammered. Justice will prevail for you, Brenda and Buster.

> **Category #2:** Interstate truck driver; the guy who's aiming that roaring eighteen-wheeler at your rear bumper. If you're not fast enough to get into the slow lane where people are only exceeding the speed limit by 10 m.p.h. and if that highway patrolman sees you closing in on that truck doing 90 m.p.h. in a 70 m.p.h. zone, **you** will get stopped—**not him!** Never forget your place, *you dummy*, driving that little Chevy Prism.

Category #3: The football, baseball, and basketball jock: Hey! We can't be too tough on these guys for a few misdemeanors like brawling, civil disobedience, drunken driving or rape. C'mon Judge, give em a break! The team needs 'em! The fans need em! What the hell! Boys will be boys.

Category #4: The elite in our society. That big shot! The well known celebrity. The people who have power, money, and clout. The same laws that would cause you to sweat for your misbehavior, those of more fortunate circumstances would fare much better.

The gavel would not resonate; the judge in a benevolent mood would cast a wink and a nod and grant forgiveness.

In a nutshell, all the laws on the books are not applied equally. Justice varies from one category to another dependent on influence and money. But take heart my fellow every man and every woman, in the good old USA, the motto is equal justice (for those with lotsa dough) under the law (as the judge feels like interpreting it that day)!

INQUIRING MINDS NEED TO KNOW

Just how pervasive is the ineptitude of our leaders in government and the private sector? When one listens to the evening news on TV, it appears to be rampant. I fully realize that good tidings do not generally make the news. Even so, the upbeat feelings one gets regarding something to cheer about is overshadowed by the gloom of our national idiosyncrasies on display day after day.

We have thousands of children killed and maimed by guns in the United States every year. Not surprising, when one considers the brain dead parents leaving loaded and unlocked guns in their homes.

There are approximately 2,000 children in Florida who are missing or unaccounted for. Their whereabouts are unknown. Post office bulletin boards across the country can attest to the enormity of this problem on a national scale.

If children go outside to play unattended or unsupervised, they are subject to the peril of falling prey to the fiends in our society from pedophiles to perverts of every imaginable description. Our national budget priorities do not provide sufficiently for children and families being protected from abuse and crime. There are more important issues, like tax cuts for the wealthy, perks for legal and illegal immigrants and bigger ball parks and stadiums for our overpaid athletes to frolic in.

What with the stock market floundering amid the pestilence of corporate fraud and chicanery menacing our whole economy and shredding investments of ordinary folks, our daily inclination toward skepticism in our governments ability to accomplish some modicum of proper leadership becomes more questionable. Now our President and Vice-President are under a cloud of suspicion regarding their past business escapades and their cozy relationships with corporate America.

The fact that our congressional leadership has a hand in questionable enterprise with all of the soft money to fund *their* campaigns and keep them in power does nothing to diminish the doubting Thomases among us.

We cannot exempt our appointed officials from the soggy ground of awkward and inappropriate conduct contributing to our beleaguered nation trying to escape from the abyss of incompetent people in positions of authority.

We have them in every sphere in our government. The most glaring examples seem to be in the judicial position of influence. Some of the decisions by these marvels of jurisprudence make the late **Judge Roy Bean** look like a Rhodes Scholar. The other organization of malfunctioning misfits can only be our own immigration department.

Last but not least, **we the plain ordinary folks** have a generous supply of homo sapiens who seem to have just emerged from the Stone Age. All those little news briefs in the daily papers keep us informed of the eccentric, strange and improper conduct contributing to the mediocrity that seems to prevail in our land.

On the front page of the *Ledger*, Polk County Florida's newspaper, we are informed of the disturbing trend of our diminishing capabilities to do anything right:

- *Hospital germs killing patients. Tens of thousands die every year because of cutbacks and carelessness, records show.*

- *Alfredo's World, did the system fail another child?*

- *Most of the Afghan civilian deaths were due to American's reliance on incomplete data.*

If incompetence is to be what we must expect, how does one cope in a society floundering with ineptitude and government agencies rife with employees indifferent and consumed with inertia when trying to resolve a problem?

The answer is: **You don't!** Not unless you are willing to sacrifice your sanity in dealing with the frustration of eternal hold, the menu choices that do not apply and all of the bureaucratic madness that impedes effective action.

DR. SAXPOT, IT'S REVOLTING!

"But, Dr. Saxpot, if what you say is true regarding Sigmund Freud's claim that sexual impulses lay at the heart of neuroses, wouldn't that be a clear indication that we are all *off our rockers* to some extent? When you consider that we humans are breaking all records for reproduction and are now contemplating cloning, what else but a species hung up on sex could be so goofy. We are the only species that has sex for fun and recreation. Based on the perspective of some talk shows, many of our congressmen and even some men of the cloth are addicted to various forms of amorous dalliance with chicks half their age."

The patient continues, "These stalwart leaders are the *noblesse oblige* in our society. If these guys have no discipline to constrain their lustful ways, how is the average serf in our kingdom gonna control his or her penchant for sexual frivolity?"

"Charles, you must remember Dr. Sigmund Freud was the first shrink. You might say the *father of psychiatry*. His theories did not necessarily mean that we humans do not possess or exhibit rational thought. Mankind is not totally occupied with sex."

"Dr. Saxpot, according to the *American Spectrum Encyclopedia*, he was reviled professionally for a decade, but the truth of his theories were finally accepted as *the real McCoy*."

"Yes Charles, but mankind's conscious intentions to himself and others are displayed by many noble deeds."

"You mean like abstaining from sex until after marriage and not watching dirty movies and staying away from girly shows and strip joints? I suppose that would even rule out lingerie fashion shows and lunches for gentlemen."

"You're missing the point, Charles. Just look at some of History's great leaders. Their accomplishments are world renowned."

"Oh, you mean guys like Henry the VIII, Louis the XVI, Napoleon and most, if not all the European big shots. Through the annals of time, they had mistresses and courtesans to dally with. And, today's British royalty, wow! Our own history is replete with philanderers and frolicking Casanovas. Dr. Saxpot, I was browsing through some magazines in our local library and I was appalled at the content of one magazine in particular, *Cosmopolitan*. Talk about sexual depravity! These are some of the decadent headings on the cover of just one issue: *Summer Bedside Astrologer; Will You Fall in Love? Or Just Lust; We've Got Your 3 Month Passion Forecast; Man Mysteries Solved—Why He Does That When He's Alone and Other Sexy Secrets He'd Never Dare Tell.* And then the Lingerie issue! Pages and pages of delicious underthings so sultry, they would make any man stutter. *Four Signs He's Whipped Over You; The Compliment Every Guy Craves; Kick These Creeps Out of Bed—You Won't Believe the Depraved, Disgusting Things These Guys Said and Did After Doing The Deed; Full View of These Panties, page 9.*"

"Charles, what attracted you to this awful magazine?"
"Research!"

DON'T BREATHE, IT COULD BE HAZARDOUS TO YOUR HEALTH

"What are you reading that you're so engrossed in, Pete? (*cough—wheeze*)."

"An article about those goofy environmentalists, the jerks, they're against everything."

Yeah, (*cough—cough*), I know what you mean, I lived by the (*wheeze*) steel mills for 35 years and the smoke and soot never bothered me (*cough—hack—cough*)."

"Ya know, Joe, just because that *one* nuclear generating plant came close to meltdown and scared a lot of people, they don't want any more nuclear plants."

"Yeah, I know them knuckleheaded (*cough—hack—wheeze—%*!@%#!*). Don't want no drilling either!"

"Joe, if we don't have gas for our S.U.V.'s, how in the Hell are we going to get around? Aw, for cryin' out loud, the traffic is really getting jammed up again."

"What, *again*? What's the problem (*cough—hack—snort*)? I'm going to miss my (*hack—hack—cough*) my flight!"

"Pete, close the windows (*hack-hack*). All that exhaust from the cars and them *!%@*!* diesel trucks is killin' me!"

"Yeah, OK, I'll put the air conditioning on."

"But, that ain't gonna keep out all the (*wheeze—cough—wheeze*) truck fumes!"

"Well what the hell do you want me to do?"

"Pull off at the next (*sneeze—wheeze—cough*) exit."

"There are already a gazillion cars and trucks lined up trying to get off—we're stuck!"

"What are you reading, now?"

"Oh, some of them environmental jerks are sayin' that if we don't stabilize our population, we'll never solve the energy crisis."

"Ah (*cough—wheeze*), what the Hell do they know?"

"Yeah, they think they're smarter than President Bush!"

"Hey, look at this. We're movin' again."

(Two hours later).

"Well, we made it to the airport, but we're an hour and a half late for your flight. Look! Your flight hasn't left yet. They haven't even started to board. You're gonna make it, Joe!"

"Jeez, there must be over 50 planes lined up on the tarmac ahead of yours. You've got plenty of time."

"So, what are you going to do when you get to your destination in Wyoming, Joe?"

"Just take it easy (*cough—hack—hack*). Just wanna get some fresh air where there ain't no cars or trucks (*wheeze—hack*), just horses. Say, I'm almost out of *Camels*. Can I borrow 50 bucks for a carton to tide me over (*hack—snort*) 'til I get to Wyoming?"

"What's that yellow (*hack—cough*) haze over there?"

"That's jet exhaust from all the planes lined up to take off."

"Are you (*hack—wheeze—snort*) OK, Pete? You look a little *woosey*."

"Yeah, I'm OK (*cough—cough*). Just got a little tickle in my throat and my eyes are watering a little (*chough—hack*)."

"Pete, you'd better try another route home. The traffic going north looked just as bad. Oh, and don't for get to stop at that new tobacco shop (*cough—wheeze—wheeze*) on Phlegm Street. They have Camels (*hack—hack*) **on sale—30% off!**"

7

Turkeys, Eagles and Endangered Species

PRESIDENTS PAST AND PRESENT

As I continue in my discourse on the madness that is becoming rampant in our sphere of influence on our planet, let me reflect on the above heading.

I was but a boy when he came on the scene, the **32nd president,** Franklin Delano Roosevelt! He was still calling the shots as I marched off to Great Lakes Naval Training Center in North Chicago, Illinois. I was still on the high seas when we, our crew, were informed of his passing. To a man, we were genuinely shocked and crestfallen when we heard the news. He was elected to an unprecedented fourth term. As a boy, I remember the mesmerizing effect his fireside chats had on my Mom and Dad, sister, brothers, and brother and sisters in law. When was the last time you were mesmerized by our recent group of turkeys? He was articulate, he had charisma, and when he addressed the nation, **he explained his policies.**

We were in the throes of a depression. People, families, (mine included), pursued any menial task to help stave off a mortgage foreclosure, and put food on the table, and heat the house. It was known as "keeping the wolf away from the door". He wove his magic and he pulled us out of our quagmire. He was a leader! When was the last time we had a leader?

President Roosevelt died during his 4th term in office and never saw the conclusion of WWII and our ultimate victory.

So Vice-president Harry S. Truman, our **33rd president** now had the challenge of ending the war. He came from humble beginnings, but proved to be an adequate leader. His most mentally burdensome decision was to use the atomic bomb on Japan to hasten the war's end. He served two terms and elected not to seek a third term.

Our **34th president,** Dwight David Eisenhower, took over the reins from Harry Truman. Eisenhower had a distinguished military career, and subsequently was made Supreme Commander of Allied forces in Europe. Upon retiring from active duty, he was appointed Supreme Commander of NATO. He and his running mate Richard Nixon defeated Adlai Stevenson and John Sparkman.

The Korean War broke out during Truman's administration, and Ike pledged to bring that conflict to an honorable end. In six months his pledge was *a fait accompli.* In 1956 he was re-elected by an over-whelming margin. He was devoted to containing communism and building a strong defense. He ordered federal troops to Little Rock, Arkansas to aid nine black children to integrate all white schools. He also signed the Civil Rights Acts of 1957 and 1960. After two terms, this very popular honorable man retired to his farm at Gettysburg, Pennsylvania.

John Fitzgerald Kennedy, our **35th president**, defeated Richard Nixon and became the youngest person and the very first Roman Catholic to attain the Presidency. He was shot in Dallas, Texas after 1,037 days in office. His legend grew after his death, concerning his youth, good looks, vigor, idealism and his supposed hanky pankee with the female gender who succumbed to his charms.

He was honored for heroism while serving in the Navy during WWII. The White House had elegant parties for artists and eggheads. He also appointed his cabinet based on the quality of gray matter between their ears. He instituted a bold new space program. He sent military advisors and military equipment to Vietnam, and allowed a

US backed invasion of Cuba, at the Bay of Pigs, which turned out to be an embarrassment for the administration.

The Cuban missile crisis caused a great deal of antagonism between the USSR and the USA. After a tense stalemate, John Kennedy prevailed and Nikita Khrushchev chickened out, and planet earth survived for another day, as the missiles were moved from Cuba. After that event, underground bombshelters became popular among the wealthy that were fond of living.

Lyndon Baines Johnson, the **36th president**, became the Chief upon the assassination of John Kennedy. As a President now in his own right, he began a program called "The Great Society for Improving US Life." Congress enacted many of his requests. The biggest issue was an unpopular and bloody war. Johnson committed more troops to the Vietnam War, which went from an advisory war under Kennedy, to a combative role. This conflict was very divisive, causing racial unrest and riots. Johnson served from November 1963 to January of 1969.

Richard Milhouse Nixon, our **37th president**, although a brilliant man, was eluded by fame and he will live in infamy as one of our biggest turkeys. He became the only President to resign from office. He faced impeachment in the wake of the Watergate scandal. As a result, he surrendered the Presidency in disgrace.

He effected important breakthroughs in the US and Chinese relations. In addition, he signed the cease-fire agreement that ended US involvement in the Vietnam War. Nixon's foreign policy achievements helped him to win re-election in 1972. He gained national recognition when he proclaimed, "I'm not a crook!"

The **38th president**, Gerald Rudolph Ford Jr., succeeded Nixon as nobleman of our realm, after the trauma that caused "tricky Dick" to be exiled to San Clemente, yo yo land. He reaffirmed US commitment to traditional US Allies. Ford made the nation's serious economic problems a top priority, but he was hampered by, what he considered, "a spend thrift Democratic Congress", perhaps angered by Ford's decision to pardon Nixon. Voters elected the next turkey!

President Ford gained fame by putting people in jeopardy when the public stood on the sidelines to watch him play golf. All things considered, he did not win many accolades for leadership. He served only one term.

The **39th president**, James Earl (Jimmy) Carter came across as a well-meaning honorable man. Carter's relations with Congress were strained. Inflation and interest rates were high during his term in office. His most significant achievement in foreign policy was a brokering of a peace treaty between Israel and Egypt in 1979. Carter's failure to win the release of 60 American hostages taken from the US Embassy in Iran by Muslim militants, led to his defeat by Ronald Reagan in the 1980 election.

Ronald Wilson Reagan, the **40th president**, became our next big enchilada on January, 1981, and served for 8 years. The Gipper could not resist calling and congratulating victorious sports figures or teams on their prowess. Being a nation of sport enthusiasts, the Gipper was readily embraced as a regular guy. The Gipper, forgot to duck, got shot by a gun nut, but survived. He strengthened our military presence in Europe, and increased support for anti-Communist forces in Central America. He signed a nuclear arms reduction treaty with the Soviet Union. Although his two terms in office brought about a temporary strong economy and cuts in federal income taxes, social programs suffered. The federal budget deficit went ballistic. An absence of contentment prevailed and some citizens wished he had stayed in Hollywood.

The **41st president**, George Herbert Walker Bush distinguished himself as a fighter pilot during WWII. He flew hazardous missions in the Pacific, earning the Distinguished Flying Cross and three air medals.

Bush's promise of no new taxes helped him attain the Presidency. He reneged on his promise, although not unknown in politics, was frowned upon by the *common folk*. Bush faced serious problems, "a legacy from Ronnie"—a huge and growing federal budget deficit, foreign trade deficits, and a financial crisis in which many savings and loan institutions required federal bail out.

The Iraqis were pushed out of Kuwait as our Allies and US forces initiated operation Desert Storm. Although he faced a series of crises, both foreign and domestic, he maintained a high level of popularity well into his third year as President. Probably his biggest media event was when the poor guy got sick and threw up at a lavish dinner during a diplomatic trek to China.

President Clinton (our **42nd president**), had a reign as *top dog* in which he can best be described as bizarre, jerk, numbskull, brilliant, stupid, immoral, and amoral. He probably fits all of these characteristics, despite the fact that he had the talent and political savvy to govern with the best of them. His apparent bent toward an amoral demeanor may very well mark him as our most dishonorable and corrupt president in our history.

His sexual misconduct and numerous scandals, abuse of power and lying all add to his infamy. I suppose that makes it a tossup between *tricky Dick* and *slick Willie*.

During his second term in office, his approval rating was high, based on a thriving economy, low unemployment, and the euphoria of a very bullish stock market and a balanced budget in the offing.

However, history will judge him, (and rightly so), on his reprehensible behavior and defilement of the highest office in the land. He will not soar with the eagles.

Despite his total lack of honor and integrity, he is held in esteem by the *boobus Americanus* elements in our land and he is vacuuming up *beaucoup* bucks to the tune of $100,000 per speech.

And now comes our **43rd president**, George W. Bush. History will judge this man! It is too early in his term to consider his leadership qualities and effectiveness at governing as our President. Many in our land, myself included, perceived him as a lightweight. Not articulate! Not intellectual! Not particularly charismatic! He personified the flaws in our political system. Despite the obvious discernible lack of high intellect and charisma, he was the recipient of immense sums of money to secure a victorious presidential campaign.

He presently holds a high approval rating by the general populous. It appears that his forte is good judgment based on common sense. He succeeded a man of intellect and charisma and no common sense, who defiled the power granted to him by the people. George W. Bush had to sweat out an extremely close vote that resulted in his opponent winning the popular vote.

The presidency of George W. Bush is perceived by many as lacking legitimacy as a result of the many and unusual *screw ups* in the electoral process in Florida and especially in the *Banana Republic of the South*, the infamous Dade County. Many citizens are of the opinion that our Commander-in-Chief gained ascendancy by a selective process, rather than an elective procedure.

8

Stand Up and Cheer!

AN ESSAY ON THE POSITIVE

Although I rail against our immigration policy, there are many who came legally, who pledge allegiance to our country, and who are worthy of our respect. The following contains an excerpt from an article published in the *Parade* magazine of the *Stuart News*:

> *In 1959 a squat bullet headed man toured our country. He was the first Soviet Premier to visit our nation. His name was Nikita Khrushchev.*
>
> *The Soviet Union and The United States were in a cold war at that time and were busy building nuclear missiles. To say the least, these were very unsettling times. Accompanying him was his son, Sergei, then a twenty-four-old missile designer, now in a country that both fascinated him and gave him pause for alarm. The threat was always present that the opposite side would start a nuclear war. Each considered the other an evil empire.*
>
> *What they saw on their visit across our land was an eye opener. They saw no soldiers in the streets. They saw Americans in their domain going about their business, and everyday tasks, and at leisure. In 1964, Nikita Khrushchev was deposed.*
>
> *After two decades, Sergei became disenchanted with the Russian bureaucracy and eagerly accepted a fellowship at the Thomas Watson Institute in Providence, R.I. He was delighted to write what he wanted without censorship.*
>
> *Now that he is an American citizen and an Ivy League professor, he reflects on why he chose U.S. citizenship.*

"I like to take care of my home," says Sergei now 65 and a senior fellow at the Thomas Watson Institute at Brown University. "It's the same with my country. I could have just stayed here with a green card, but my wife and I decided to be responsible, to live here, to vote, not just to consume. It's not political or ideological; it's personal. I feel very proud to be in this country".

He teaches at Brown University and at the Naval War College, (a school for military officers). Sergei and his wife Valentina, 53, a home-maker, were sworn in as U.S. citizens in Providence on July 12, 1999.

Sergei is the personification of an immigrant ready and willing to accept our culture, become an American and contribute to our country's needs. Welcome, Sergei and Valentia!

TREE WOMAN GAVE US A HEROIC LESSON

Lest we forget, we do have something to cheer about. I will include some uplifting themes at times to alleviate depression. Many young people and some adults view their favorite athletes as heroes. While many do represent themselves as good role models, heroes they are not.

Julia "Butterfly" Hill is the representation of the essence of heroism. This young woman withstood the elements of nature by living in a towering, ancient redwood tree for two years to save it from a logger's chainsaw:

To motor in the Pacific Northwest and be in awe of these magnificent forests and then round a curve and see a mountainside denuded of trees, will numb the senses of all but the most blase to our environment.

Without people like Julia, God only knows what our planet would become. For every Julia we have scores of litterbugs. We have vandals who call themselves loggers (granted, there are some loggers who practice responsible forestry methods). We have corporations whose hauteur toward the environment is only exceeded by some politicians who pander to their special interests.

Hats off to Julia and her kind. Ours is the only planet in our solar system blessed with diverse beauty and life. Thanks to Julia, we have a wake-up call to realize how precious this jewel, our "planet Earth" is.

The sad part of this scenario is the fact that it takes such nobility of spirit by one person to achieve a goal to preserve some of our natural beauty.

TWO HEROES IN OUR MIDST

Florida is the habitat of two species of wildlife known for their voracious desire to feast upon human flesh if the opportunity presents itself. These frightful occurrences are becoming more prevalent in the realm these creatures call home.

Gators and sharks are the culprits. By their malevolent behavior they are gaining in infamy. The problem takes place when people cavort in their backyard. The hue and cry is, "Why is this happening so often?" Ultimately some seer out there tries to enlighten the rest of us dummies that if the sharks and gators are hungry, these brutes will do what is natural and sample the tidbits presented to them. Common sense tells us that increasing numbers of people frolicking in the lakes, rivers and surf put pressure on the habitat of the *people eaters.*

The heroics in this instance took place in the surf near Pensacola, Florida. A Mr. Vance Flosenzier accomplished an extraordinary feat. Jessie Arbogast and his Uncle Vance were enjoying the surf in relatively shallow water when terror struck near dusk in the form of a 200 pound, 7 foot bull shark. Jessie, an 8-year-old lad first sustained a deep bite in his thigh. Then the shark went for his right arm and held fast. The subsequent events are nothing short of miraculous. Uncle Vance achieved something few people could, or would attempt. He wrestled that 200-pound shark on the beach. His courageous act made it possible for the shark to be shot and Jessie's arm to be recovered from the shark's jaw. Jessie lost a profuse amount of blood. At this writing, he is in stable condition, with his arm reattached with a good chance of recovery.

Heroic deeds by people are not uncommon when the need arises.

None, however, could quite match the valiant effort of the shark fighter with the exception, maybe of this tough little canine.

On Friday, July 27, 2001, an article in our local newspaper told of another heroic deed by man's best friend, Blue, a 2 year-old Australian blue healer.

> *Ruth Gay, an 85 year-old woman, fell while walking her dog Blue. The dog lay by her side, but suddenly started to growl and left. It was dark. She knew her scrappy little 35 pound dog was in a fight. He was fending off an alligator emerging from a canal 50 feet from Gay's home. Blue sustained numerous puncture wounds fending off that gator, but his heroics enabled Gay's son-in-law to come to her aid. He became aware that something was wrong with Blue's barking and yelping. Ruth Gay is in fair condition in a Fort Myers hospital and Blue is recovering after being treated at an animal hospital.*

Kudos to Blue as he licks his wounds!

SOMETHING TO CHERISH

Lorraine and I received a letter from our grandson and our granddaughter today that pretty much exemplifies that our land, our culture, our society has a full share of people dedicated to the virtue of giving and caring. Living as we are, often beset in a climate of chaos and instability, that we have among us many people who make us aware of the dedication to all that is good and meaningful still exists in our country This letter to grandma and grandpa can attest to that commitment. As long as we have people who manifest a spirit of good will, there is hope.

> *Dear Family & Friends:*
>
> *It has been a month since the Avon 3-day 60-mile walk, which has allowed us time to reflect on all of the wonderful moments. We want to*

thank you again for your financial and emotional support all along the way. The Dallas Avon 3-Day raised over 2 million dollars for breast cancer research and early detection programs and we achieved almost 200% of our pledge goal due to your generous contribution.

There were so many special moments during the event that will stay with us always. The Opening Ceremony in Keller, TX with all of our anticipation, laid a wonderful foundation to give us the will to go on even when it got rough. We walked by an elementary school about 45 minutes into our first day The school allowed all of the students to stand at the fence and cheer us on with signs like "Go Girls" and "You Can Do It!" Although the weather all three days was not very cooperative (rain, extreme humidity, wind), we learned to adapt our clothing quickly. We completed our 20 miles on Day One at Grapevine Lake. I walked with a wonderful couple from Austin (Chris and Lisa Marie) that Ryan and I met at our hotel. They continued throughout the event to be our meal and entertainment companions. It was easy to meet many wonderful people along the way.

Day Two took us from Grapevine to Richardson. The crew was extremely helpful at every stop along the way providing drinks, snacks, and encouragement. What was so touching were all of the friends and family along the way giving encouragement to all who passed. My best friend, Sylvia, even came to the camp that night to enjoy the evening entertainment and check out our accommodations. Although Ryan and I don't usually choose camping vacations, it was a lot of fun. We had hot showers, clean portable toilets, and a fairly comfortable tent.

Day Three (our last day) took us from Richardson to the campus of Southern Methodist University in Dallas for our Closing Ceremony. It was the hottest day, but after completing two days, there was no giving up. As I crossed the finish line, there were hundreds of people cheering. Ryan, as part of the stage crew, had already reached the finish and was waiting to give me big hug. The picture above was taken at the finish receiving our special shirts to wear for the Closing Ceremony, which had to be the most emotional part of the entire three days. First to come into the stadium were most of the 3-day walkers (in blue shirts). We were shortly followed by those in pink shirts who not only completed the walk, but had overcome a greater challenge—surviving breast cancer. The crew entered last so that everyone could thank them for volunteering to give up three days to ensure that the wallkers were pampered.

They truly worked harder than all, even the walkers. On all sides of the stadium were family and friends who came to commemorate our accomplishment. Mike and Sylvia even brought ice cream (the really good stuff) for Ryan, our friends from Austin and myself.

Although it took a few days to recuperate from the physical strain of the event, both of us were glowing from the incredible kindness and strength we experienced. We will be forever changed by it. Thank you again for your contribution, which allowed us to participate in such an incredible event and for those life will be forever changed by it.

A TIME FOR REFLECTION

The art of poetry, though not dead has diminished in this day and age. Poetry has its place with people of all ages. To the poets of today, we praise you for your efforts to keep alive the magic of your lyrics.

It seems such a simple thing to compose; yet it is not! I believe it must be a gift, bestowed on a few who possess a feel of romantic imagery usually fancifully depicted. The beauty of poetry can be conveyed in lyrical form regarding nature, legend, romantic love, platonic love—in short, many of the simple treasures in short supply these days.

The lyrical verse of a simple poem can captivate the senses and, "soothe the savage beast."

"To be praised is to be honored."

"To be loved is the greatest gift."

"Love is expressed in many ways."

Love is a dominant force and pervades through our extended family. Our son-in-law has the gift of expressing love in poetry. Let me share his gift with you.

Ode to an Old Salt

Bask in the light of fatherhood, for this is your day of gold;
A dad sometimes stern, but a heart of tenderness if truth be told.

Your children now grown, with kids of their own,
Were stones in the pond where ripples now roam.

Time has passed and years flee away,
But memories are such that hold for this day.

With toil and trouble we ask why all the bother?
Until a card that you open—happy day, my father!

On The 54th Anniversary of our Marriage

Pages blank, chapters unknown,
Seeds that sprout, chances sown.

Loves blended, the sum more than two;
Love that has grown, love that is true.

Memories, ah memories, stories of gold;
We live them through you, so often told.

Now more to write, the inkwell stands yet;
New days are dawning, more memories to get.

Ode to a Birthday Girl

On a cold winter's night way back in '54,
Lorraine and Charles were walking the floor.

She, very calm, thought obvious in distress;
Dear old dad was probably a mess.

Then off with a suitcase sat close by the door,
And hopefully the car was warmed up before.

Tracing the route both had laid out;
Hoping the car wouldn't crap out.

Prompted by nature that isn't a joke,
Lorraine said, "Hurry, my water just broke!"

Then off to delivery with rush and a whirl,
Waiting with wonder, a boy or a girl?

Now time for mother, she only can labor,
While Dad waits outside, a moment to savor.

When out of the breech, the moment arrives,
Squirming and crying, so very much alive.

So marvelous a sight, so tiny and pink,
A daughter it was, now what did they think?

Fast forward now those 45 years;
Those filled with joy and yes, lots of tears.

Toil and trouble and forks in the road,
But you had help to shoulder the load.

A mother yourself, you've done the drill;
Nothing can alter the memories, the thrill.

When great with child, your tummy of girth;
You know what it's like, the miracle of birth.

What lies ahead, you truly can't say,
But one thing for sure: This is your day!

Here is the beautiful simplicity of a puzzling subject—life!

Life
by Lizette Woodworth Reese

Glad that I live am I,
That the sky is blue;
Glad for the country lanes,
And the fall of dew.

After the sun, the rain,
After the rain, the sun;
This is the way of life,
'Till the work be done.

All that we need to do,
Be we low or high,
Is to see that we grow
Nearer to the sky.

Sweet, simple, significant—if you can read between the lines. In this technological age, it seems too many of us find too little time to read between the lines.

In Summary

Many years ago when Lorraine and I called the Chicago area our home, Jack Mabley wrote a column in a Chicago newspaper. His column on one occasion foretold of his thoughts regarding the proliferation of nuclear weapons and the peril associated with an unrestrained human population. His reasoning was some nutcase will eventually get a nuclear weapon or weapons and—well you get the picture.

So, here we are facing the fear we are loath to think about. With a populous of teeming billions inhabiting planet earth, the ratio of "nutcases" increases in direct proportion to the number of people straining our resources.

Should the good guys prevail and halt the ever-present danger of Armageddon, we still have the problem of how to cope with our planets burgeoning human population.

Picture for a moment someone from Asia, Africa, or South America who has been in residence in our country for the last four or five years. Perhaps as a student in one of our universities or employed here. He or she then goes back home, (which most would never consider) for a brief period, or permanently.

They are now aware of the glaring obsession in our culture of the most, the biggest, the best and our insatiable lust for worldly goods and possessions that constitute the pinnacle of our life's values. What better example than the incomprehensible greed of most of the corporate executives of some of our biggest companies. Add to that the terrible adverse impact of the recent disclosures of "cooking the books" and outright theft by these "big shots", and leaving the workers and investor's holding the bag. Now we have a ripple effect on the economy and lack of trust; the direct result of their lust for money.

Now these wayfarers are back home, enlightening their less privileged countrymen on our excesses. They get the whole shot! "Hey Chang, Ummgaawa, and Juan and Rosalita did you know that just a few of the richest men in American could provide the people of our country with food and clean drinking water for five years."

"Hey, I hear dos peeples in America got bad health cus dey too fat."

"Yes, that's right, Umgaawa, some are so fat, they cannot walk much. "They drive around on battery powered carts."

"What do dey eat, dey get so fat?"

"The most, the biggest, and the best of everything."

Next they are given the lowdown on democracy in action. President Bush is now the topic of discussion.

"Carumba!" "President Bush—he speaks Spanish that help him be elected President?"

"Well that was a help Juan, but what helps the most in America is who has the most money." Bush had the most big and biggest bucks." That was why he was chosen."

"Ho-ho!" "What if smart guy wants to be President in U.S.A. but has no big bucks?"

"No chance Chang, not in America.,

So, where the Hell are we? We keep telling ourselves that we're the greatest.

What constitutes our greatness? Is it the fact that we possess so much wealth? We have the most millionaires and most billionaires. Many amassed their wealth by devious means and by the lotteries so prevalent in our country.

Let's face it; we're at the top of the heap in consumerism. We beat out every one on the planet in every category of our demands for more, more, and still more. The result is evident on the overwhelming waste we generate. "Yessiree, Bob!" "We're the greatest!" Is it any wonder we're perceived as arrogant, and the "Ugly American," by increasing numbers of those foreigners.

Perhaps our greatness stems from generosity! We pump untold sums of taxpayers' money into foreign aid that usually ends up providing more luxuries for the creeps in positions of power while the little emaciated guy "sucks hind tit." Or how about the many privileges granted to legal and illegal aliens while many Americans cannot afford proper healthcare or sorely needed medication, and in many instances go to bed hungry.

At any rate, "Dear Reader," I believe my essays tell the story of a lifetime of observation regarding the country I cherish. The winds of change have gone from subtle to abrupt in my country's leaders in their seemingly negligent choice of priorities in setting a proper course for, "our ship of state." I have tried to put together a synopsis of the characteristics of the changes I have seen in my countrymen and women and in most instances to the detriment of my country's esteem.

I feel that I have only scratched the surface of the nuances in our society that have regressed, in many instances, to displeasing and obnoxious behavior.

At this writing, we are closing in on our annual 4th of July celebration, in the year 2002. I will leave you with this final thought. Many people of all age groups will be watching in awe of that fireworks display. If you were to ask the question of anyone, or to a group in attendance at this event, "What is the significance of our celebration today?"

I would be curious to know, how many blank stares you would get, especially among the young.

0-595-25670-8

www.ingramcontent.com/pod-product-compliance
Lightning Source LLC
Chambersburg PA
CBHW020303290526
45784CB00003B/1345